BITTER FRUIT

ROD BROOME

ISIS
LARGE PRINT
Oxford

First published in Great Britain 2010
by
ISIS Publishing Ltd.

Published in Large Print 2010 by ISIS Publishing Ltd.,
7 Centremead, Osney Mead, Oxford OX2 0ES
by arrangement with
The Author

All rights reserved

The moral right of the author has been asserted

British Library Cataloguing in Publication Data
Broome, Rod, 1937–
     Bitter fruit. - - (Reminiscence)
     1. Broome, Rod, 1937–
     2. Teachers - - England - - Biography.
     3. Elementary school principals - - England - -
     Biography.
     4. Large type books.
     I. Title II. Series
     371.1'0092–dc22

ISBN 978–0–7531–9582–6 (hb)
ISBN 978–0–7531–9583–3 (pb)

Printed and bound in Great Britain by
T. J. International Ltd., Padstow, Cornwall

For Anita

Please return / renew by date shown.
You can renew it at:
norlink.norfolk.gov.uk
or by telephone: 0344 800 8006
Please have your library card & PIN ready

12/12

JUL 23

12 SEP 23

OCT 23

27.

BITTER FRUIT

Introduction

In my second book, *Branching Out*, I described how, after two very enjoyable years at a Manchester teacher training college, I finally qualified and began to make my way in the world.

The first twelve months of my career proved to be highly eventful. I was appointed to teach at a junior school in a "working class" area of the city; I succumbed to a nasty dose of pneumonia caused — everyone said — by living in a cold, damp, rented flat; and on Christmas Eve, I became engaged to Anita, the most wonderful girl in the world!

I had met Anita at College, and within months we were deeply in love and making wedding plans. Our marriage took place on 1ˢᵗ April 1961 in Cheetham Hill Methodist Church.

We found a small terraced house in Sudden, a suburb of Rochdale and little by little made friends with our neighbours and the local shop owners. A year or two later, we bought an elderly Austin car, decided to start a family and moved all of 500 yards to a semi-detached bungalow, which was part of a small estate recently built in a field formerly attached to Marland Hill Farm. Married life seemed to suit us well, and we were happy together.

The year after I began teaching there, Alfred Street Boys' School in Harpurhey was merged with the Girls'

School to become Harpur Mount Junior School under the headship of Miss Nora Bottoms.

The merger went well, and I liked and respected Miss Bottoms. I continued to teach Junior Two children (eight-year-olds), refereed football matches against neighbouring schools, and generally played my part as a member of the staff. After four years, Miss Bottoms retired to be replaced by Mrs Joyce Earl, who promoted me first to Teacher/Librarian and then Head of English Department. In that post, I set about reorganising the school reading scheme, a task I relished as I recognized that the ability to read well was the key to success for many children. My aim was to ensure that children could progress at their optimum speed to the top of their ability level, rather than be held back (or put under pressure) by limited resources. At work everything in the garden was lovely. I felt valued and respected by the other members of staff and enjoyed teaching the children from working-class homes — believing I was making a real difference to their lives.

However, the time came when I began to think I ought to be moving on. Several younger teachers who had joined the staff after me had already moved to senior positions in other schools, and I recognised that I was not just getting into a rut, but was in danger of putting down a tap root! So when a job came up at a large school in Rochdale, I decided to take the plunge.

The account that follows records events accurately (to the best of my knowledge), but I have changed the names of all the schools, the governors, the teachers, ancillary workers, parents and children to protect the innocent!

PART ONE

CHAPTER
ONE

A Change of Scene

In the Spring term of 1968, I applied to become Head of English Department at Kempsell Junior School in Rochdale. It was a large red-brick building within a couple of miles of my home, and I was attracted by the shorter journey time and the fact that its summer holiday pattern had been planned to include the Rochdale "Wakes Week", when all the cotton mills shut down, and many people headed for the coast. For several years I had been at work when most Rochdale people were enjoying their annual holiday, and on holiday when our friends and neighbours were out at work.

The post I was applying for was equivalent to the one I already held at Harpur Mount Junior, but as the school had many more children, I thought that my scope for personal development would be greater. I completed my application form, attended for interview, and was delighted to be told that I had got the job.

Reality hit me on the first morning when the Head Teacher informed me that my main duties as Head of English would be to:

- keep a check on the number of lined exercise books in stock and tell the deputy head when more were needed
- make sure there was always an adequate supply of soap and paper towels in the cloakrooms
- supervise the children as they washed their hands before lunch
- take my turn at refereeing Saturday morning football matches

I was to have no responsibility for the assessment or choice of reading materials; I would not be advising teachers coming against specific reading problems in the classroom; and I certainly had no role in planning the English curriculum.

That first morning, I also recognised that I felt uneasy about the general ambience within the school. It had the feeling of a large impersonal institution. I was to learn later that amongst Rochdale teachers it had the nickname of "the factory".

The Head Teacher, Ted Cartwright, was an ex-army officer who ran everything with military precision. Although, on the surface, he appeared fairly genial, I soon learned that his leadership lacked the warmth and encouragement I had appreciated at Harpur Mount. At regular intervals throughout the day, he would stalk the corridors between classrooms, peering over the glass partitions as if to make instant judgement on what was happening within. This constant scrutiny gave me the impression that the Head was on the lookout for any negative situation on which he could pounce.

Whether it was his military demeanour (I had hated National Service!) or the bad "vibes" I had picked up on that first morning I don't know, but I returned home after my very first day to tell Anita that I hated the new job and intended to move on at the first opportunity!

Anita had left teaching when our son was born in 1965 and had taken on the role of housewife. She enjoyed doing all the things that other women seemed to grumble about — cooking, cleaning, shopping, and even the often-dreaded ironing. She enjoyed, too, meeting other young Mums at the shops or the baby clinic.

Now she stared at me in amazement as I made my statement.

"But you've only been there for one day," she reasoned. "You've got to give it longer than that!"

I knew that Anita had a point, but during subsequent days my initial impressions were confirmed. By the end of that first week, I had made up my mind that my stay at the school would be as short as possible. I had discovered that teachers were hedged in by petty rules that restricted their professionalism and creativity.

At Harpur Mount, if a teacher needed more exercise books, paper or paint, they would ask the Deputy Head for the stockroom key at playtime, get what they required, and return the key to him afterwards. That was considered far too free and easy for Kempsell! A "stock book" had to be kept by each teacher who would hand it in to Mrs Kernick, the Deputy Head, every Thursday morning with a list of stock required during the following seven days. The materials were duly distributed on Friday, and woe betide anyone who had forgotten to include an essential item!

One always felt that one was being "checked up on". For instance, one of my duties — supervising the children as they washed their hands before lunch — meant that I had to rush to the cloakroom each day as soon as the mid-day bell rang. If I were delayed by having to deal with a child in my class and arrived a few minutes late, I would find Ted Cartwright there before me, who would make it quite clear that I had fallen down on my duty.

Kempsell Junior School was the only school in which I worked where paper staplers were numbered and signed out to each teacher — if one went missing, it was quite clear who was to blame!

I had been appointed to the school in May 1968 and knew that I would have to remain there for at least a year — so I gritted my teeth and counted down to the New Year when I would be able to apply for other jobs.

In the Spring Term of 1969, I began to scour the educational press for suitable vacancies in local primary schools. I had redefined the word "local" during the previous months and was quite willing to travel a considerable distance in order to free myself from the restrictive regime of Kempsell Junior. A daily journey of 20 miles over the Pennines into Yorkshire or a 40 minute drive through the Trough of Bowland into the heart of rural Lancashire now seemed quite acceptable in my desperate search for an escape route.

I was applying for deputy headships. Although I had been employed in only two schools since qualifying, I had worked under four Head Teachers, had ten years teaching experience and had been promoted twice. I must admit that I felt somewhat self-conscious asking Ted Cartwright for a reference after working in his school for less than a year, but I bit the bullet and did my best to give him the impression that I was very ambitious and, as my present post was similar to my previous one, I was looking for fresh challenges. He willingly agreed to write a reference for me if one was requested by a local authority to which I had applied.

The long search began! Each week I would pour over the *Times Educational Supplement* and send off for forms from Local Authorities. Then, long before the days of computers, I was faced with the time-consuming procedure of filling in boxes, writing letters of application detailing my ten years experience, and contacting possible referees. Once completed, I would dispatch my application with a hope and a prayer.

Successful applicants usually heard if they had been shortlisted within a couple of weeks, when they would be told the date and time of the interview. Those not shortlisted would get a letter after about three or four weeks saying that the post had been filled.

In those days the interviewing of teachers — including Deputy Heads — was held after the school day had finished, often on a Friday evening. The interviewing panel would usually consist of the Head

Teacher, an educational advisor, a representative of the local authority, and a number of school managers (now governors), some of whom were local councillors.

The Head and Educational Advisor would ask a number of "educational" questions, often referring to the letter sent in by the applicant, whilst the school managers seemed to ask anything that came into their minds! Questions such as, "What would you do if the school was flooded?" or "How would you capture a stray horse in the playground?" were not uncommon!

Attending interviews for deputy headships soon became quite a social occasion. I would arrive at a school for interview, be shown into a waiting room and find myself in the company of the same group of men and women I had been with on a previous occasion two weeks before. We were all on the "shortlist" circuit — and apart from the successful candidate who would not reappear, we would all say farewell until the next occasion!

After about half a dozen of these "reunions", however, I was beginning to feel I had had enough of them. Several times, I was sure that I had had a really good interview, only to discover later that once again I had not been given the job. I was bemoaning my fate to Anita when she suggested that I might try changing one of my referees. He was an older teacher who had been a colleague at Harpur Mount. He had developed the habit of dropping in to see us, accompanied by his wife, on Sunday evenings after church. Although to me he always appeared friendly and supportive, Anita had

8

picked up the "vibes" that he was a little jealous of my progress. And as she is very intuitive I took her advice!

In September 1969, I filled out my ninth application form for a deputy headship at Turnbrook Way Primary School in Readburn, near Oldham. It was within a few miles of Oldham town centre, but fell just outside the Oldham Borough boundary. So rather than being an Oldham school, Turnbrook Way came under "Lancashire, Division 23", which was run by its own divisional educational officer and administrative staff.

The school was a single-storey red-brick building with high windows and a front entrance on the main road. Behind the building was a large, walled playground, a piece of open grassland and a football pitch. It was a one form entry school, having three infant and four junior classes, and it was only a 20 minute drive from home.

On the appointed Friday evening, I took my turn, along with five other applicants, to go into the head's study to face the panel. I was fortunate in having a surname beginning with "B" as candidates were usually summoned in alphabetical order, and I got my ordeal over quickly. I did not think I had done particularly well this time, so I was astounded when the Educational Advisor emerged from the room at the end of the interview procedure to call me in again. It was the custom for the successful candidate to be offered the post before the other applicants were sent away — possibly to allow for the fact that the "chosen one" may have changed his mind!

I was delighted to accept the position and was told to give in my notice at Kempsell Junior as soon as possible in order to take up my new post when the Spring Term began in January. The head of the school, Mr Raymond Handforth, was a short man with a pinched face, flushed cheeks and thin purple hands. He congratulated me warmly, fixed me with his dark, beady eyes and told me I would be taking the "top class" — Junior 4 children, who would be sitting their 11+ examination just a month or two after I took up my post.

"We always do very well, here," he said pointedly. "The 11+ examination is high on our list, and we always get a good number through to Grammar School."

It did not seem appropriate to mention the fact that, as a child, I had failed the 11+ the first time I took it, or that I thought that laying emphasis on the exam caused a great deal of distress to some children. Neither did I say that although it might boost the confidence of those children who passed, children who were unsuccessful and went to a Secondary Modern School were often left with a real sense of failure. But, I was pleased to have got the job and thought it wiser to keep these opinions to myself.

Anita was as delighted as I was that the job was mine, if only to bring an end to my continual moaning about Ted Cartwright! During supper, I went over the interview with her, trying to remember all the questions I had been asked and recall the answers I had given. At last things were looking up. I had only a few more weeks to endure at Kempsell Junior, and then I would be making a fresh start in a new school — and what is more, I would be in the elevated position of Deputy Head Teacher.

CHAPTER
TWO

The Deep End

The Christmas holiday of 1969 was a particularly enjoyable one. I had shaken hands with the head and staff at Kempsell Junior and was looking forward to my new job at Turnbrook Way Primary School. Although an experienced teacher, there would be one age-range of children there that I had never taught — infants, aged 4 to 7 years.

At the time I qualified, most young children began their school lives in separate Infant Schools, with "Infant" Heads, and after three years transferred to Junior Schools under "Junior" Heads. In common with many male teachers, I had worked only in junior schools, and was not used to dealing with *very* young children. However, the new Primary Schools brought both age groups together under one roof. Seeing small children about the school was going to be a new experience for me. One of the infant teachers at Turnbrook Way would have special responsibility for the running of the infant department whilst I, as Deputy Head, would be at the other end of the scale, teaching the "top class", Junior 4.

I went into school on a few days before the Spring Term began to sort out my classroom and weigh up equipment. I was able to get to know Mr Wilson, the elderly caretaker who I found polishing the hall floor, but I was disappointed that none of the other members of staff were around as I had yet to meet any of them. I expected Mr Handforth would introduce me to them all on the first day of term.

The big day arrived. It was a cold January morning as I gave Anita an enthusiastic wave, got into the car, and drove off in the direction of Oldham. I arrived in good time — around 8.20a.m. — and walked through the front door and into the staffroom. The room felt quite familiar to me as it had been the waiting room for interviewees several weeks earlier. It was deserted, so I crossed the corridor to the Head's room, only to discover that that too was unoccupied and moreover, it was locked and in darkness.

Returning to the staff room, I sat in an armchair and waited. Over the next fifteen minutes several members of staff arrived, and rather self-consciously I introduced myself to each in turn. All were women and, as they all knew each other, the room was alive with conversation. They exchanged news of how they had spent the holiday: their preparations for Christmas Day, the presents they had received from family and friends, and the New Year parties they had been to. I sat in silence, feeling a bit like a spare part. From time to time I went to the staff room door to check the room opposite. It was still in darkness — Mr Handforth had still not arrived!

At last, I heard a key turning in a lock and shot to the door once more only to find a petite, well-dressed woman going into the Head's room. I hurriedly introduced myself and discovered that she was Mrs Batley, the school secretary.

"Do you know where Mr Handforth is?" I asked anxiously, but she shook her head.

"I've only just arrived," she answered. "He's usually here by now."

I looked at my watch and saw that it was almost nine o'clock. I knew I had to take action. Returning to the staff room, I broke into the conversation.

"Can you tell me what happens when the bell goes?" I asked. "It doesn't look as though Mr Handforth is coming."

A tall thin teacher, who had introduced herself as Miss Butterfield, smiled reassuringly.

"Oh don't worry — the children go into class first and we all do the registers," she said. "Then — about ten past nine — everyone goes into the hall for assembly."

Assembly! My heart leapt as I suddenly realised that in the Head's absence, it was the Deputy's role to take morning assembly.

"What do you do in assembly?" I gulped, knowing that all schools tended to do things differently.

"Oh, we just sing a song and have a prayer, and then Mr Handforth usually says a word or two. Don't worry about it. We'll sing 'Morning has broken' — they all know that one. And we could just say the Lord's Prayer . . ."

In that moment I realised that Miss Butterfield must be the school pianist. I smiled at her and tried to look unconcerned — even nonchalant — but as the bell sounded and I hurried into my classroom, my heart was thumping.

Until the very last second before I walked out in front of the 240 children and 7 members of staff, I was hoping against hope that Mr Handforth would suddenly appear and apologise for oversleeping! But it was not to be.

"Good morning, everyone," I said, making my first mistake. As the children launched into their automatic chanted response, I realised that they didn't know my name.

"Good morning, Mr Han . . . (mumble mumble), good morning everyone."

"Well, you're probably very surprised to see me here. My name is Mr Broome, and I'm going to be teaching Primary 4 from now on. Mr Handforth isn't here this morning, but that gives me a good chance to meet you all. Now, let me see how well you can sing . . . It's hymn number . . ."

Miss Butterfield struck the first note on the piano and 240 children declared that morning had broken, and praised God for it. The Lord's Prayer followed and, after I had said a few words about the New Year, and

15

making New Year resolutions, the children filed out of the hall. Somehow I had got over the first hurdle!

Once in my classroom, I was on more familiar territory, and began to organise things to my liking, but the fact that Mrs Batley frequently popped in with questions: "Will you sign the dinner-money book?", "There's a traveller here; shall I tell him to go away?" etc., kept the fact that I was in charge of the school firmly in the front of my mind.

Just before playtime, she appeared again.

"I've just had Mrs Handforth on the phone," she said. "Mr Handforth isn't going to make it today — he isn't at all well. He hopes to be in tomorrow morning."

I thanked her for the message and carried on teaching, passing on the information to the staff at playtime, whilst trying to appear unfazed by fact that I knew nothing about the school's routine or organization.

I went through the rest of the day relying to a large extent on the advice of those around me. I dutifully signed a number of papers put in front of me by Mrs Batley and asked various teachers how things were usually done. For example, the school meal at lunchtime was cooked in a large secondary school just across the road, but I needed to know how it was brought to our building and how it was served in our school hall. The children in my class needed to change for P.E., but I was not sure whether this was done in the classroom (as it was in many schools) or whether the girls retired to the cloakroom to protect their modesty.

My whole day was fraught with uncertainty. Although everyone was most helpful, I admit that I breathed a sigh of relief when the bell signalled that it was time to go home. I had coped well under the circumstances, but looked forward to the return to normality on the following morning.

As I retold the events of the day to Anita that evening, everything took on a humorous slant. It became a comical tale of how chaos had reigned and how I, like Mr Bean, had blundered from one disaster to another.

"Well, at least there was a happy ending," she said. "You were thrown in at the deep end, but you didn't sink, you swam."

"Well, it was more like floating really," I replied. "I'm glad I don't have to go through that again!"

But unfortunately I did. The start of the second day in school was an action replay of the first one, with the Head not turning up, and Mrs Handforth ringing in well after 9 o'clock to say he was not well. This time, however, the experience was less traumatic as at least I knew the staff, and a little of the day-to-day routine. I returned home that night with more confidence in my ability to survive.

On day three, I went into school fully prepared to take the helm yet again, only to find Mr Handforth in occupation and in a commanding mood. Without mention of his absence, he began to tell me how things should be done and introduced me to his priorities for the school.

They were:

- Getting as many children as possible through the 11+ examination
- Making sure that everything was done in an orderly way.

My duties included working out the teachers' playground supervision rota and arranging for cover when there were staff absentees. In addition, I was responsible for ordering stock and sets of BBC pamphlets, produced to accompany radio broadcasts for schools. One of the more memorable programmes was "Singing Together" with William Appleby, who welcomed everyone each week with the greeting "Hello, schools!" and led a twenty-minute programme in which the children learned traditional songs such as "Bobby Shaftoe" and "The Ashgrove".

On one afternoon each week, I took the older boys for "Games" — which meant football — and being the only man on the staff, I selected the school football team and refereed home matches, which took place after 4p.m. on the pitch behind the playground. Mr Handforth was quite keen on our team winning, although I noticed that he never came out to stand on the touchline and cheer us on.

However, the reason for this soon became apparent — Mr Handforth was not a well man. During the spring term of 1970 he was absent from school many times — a day or two every couple of weeks — and this pattern continued into the summer.

At school, I had noticed that he was a heavy smoker, and, when I went into his room, he would often be standing in a haze of cigarette smoke in front of the window, looking out and taking deep breaths. Occasionally, he would complain about the "moor-grime" (mist) which hung over the local hills, and blame it for preventing him from "getting his breath". In retrospect, remembering his hunched shoulders, pinched face, hollow cheeks and purple hands, I feel sure that he was suffering from emphysema, but at the time I knew nothing about the illness.

As the months passed, although I had learned to cope with the uncertainty which each morning might bring, I still found the Head's unpredictable absences unsettling. Fortunately, Mrs Batley had everything under control in the school office, so when Mr Handforth didn't arrive we all carried on regardless and there were few occasions when things went seriously wrong. The staff was very cooperative and would always help out if a difficult situation arose, and yet there was a sense in which the school appeared to be continually marking time, rather than making progress. There were few opportunities to consider new initiatives or introduce fresh ideas into the school.

In late spring, we held the usual parents' evening, and a great many parents came in to see me. The one question on all their lips was, "Has she/he got any chance of getting through?" They were referring, of course, to the 11+ examination, and it was difficult to know how to answer them. I had set one or two practice papers during the previous weeks and had a pretty good idea which children would be progressing

19

to Grammar School, but there was no way of being sure — and I was very unhappy to go along with many parents' view that those who "did not make it" were failures. I kept promoting the idea that the test was designed to select which secondary school was *most suitable for their child*, but I could see it did not carry much weight.

I was even more disillusioned with the system when the results came and I realised how the places at Grammar School were allocated. Let us imagine that there were ninety places available at the local grammar school. Examination papers would be marked and a line drawn under the ninetieth child on the list — those who were above the line would get a place; those below the line would fail to do so. No account was taken from year to year of the *actual marks* gained by the children, so a mark which took a child above the line in one year might not be good enough to get a child into grammar school in the following year. There was in fact no pass mark as such — whether one "succeeded" or "failed" depended on the brightness or otherwise of the group of children who sat the exam that year!

As the summer holiday approached we had the usual end of term events — school reports were issued, a sports day was held and day-visits to their new schools were arranged for our children who were transferring to secondary schools in September. Our infant department welcomed in the young children (and parents) who were to be admitted to our reception class after the summer holiday. They came in a few at a time on successive days to meet the reception class teacher and get used to the school environment.

And so the year drew to an end. Although my introduction to Turnbrook Way had not been easy, I had made a good start. During my first two terms as deputy head I had worked well with the staff and been able to cope in unpredictable and variable circumstances. I was looking forward to the six week summer break when I could relax with Anita and our own children. Hopefully, the next year would run more smoothly and life would be a little easier.

CHAPTER
THREE

Into the Breach

Whilst I was out in the big wide world pursuing my career, Anita was content to stay at home with our lively toddler son and our beautiful baby daughter. It was great for me, after a busy day at school, to return home to a warm house, a tasty meal and a relaxing evening in the bosom of my family.

Although I played my part in the home, I was in no way a "new man". I never ironed my shirts or cooked a meal, nor did I wash any clothes nor clean the bathroom. In those days this was not considered at all reprehensible, and in my defence I would say that I installed central heating, wallpapered and painted rooms, built numerous cupboards and wardrobes, and maintained the garden — not to mention regularly servicing our little car, something that it was quite possible to do in simpler times. My proud boast was that I saved the family a fortune with my DIY activities!

At weekends, in common with many parents of young children, we fitted in visits to grandparents and spent a lot of time in the local park pushing the little ones on swings or kicking a football around.

In 1965, at the age of 61, my father decided that he would like to be able to drive, so he bought a second hand Morris Minor and looked around for someone to teach him. Although there were several private driving instructors in the area working from their own homes, in those days many people were taught by members of their own family. The previous year, Anita had sailed through her test at the first attempt under my tuition, so I volunteered to take on my father as a pupil. He must have presented a comical sight as he climbed into the driving seat wearing his trilby hat with his favourite briar pipe clenched tightly between his teeth. To our delight he passed the test at his second attempt, thereby giving him — and Mum — greater freedom to visit their grandchildren more often and to explore "pastures new" in their retirement.

One day in 1971, Anita received a phone call with an offer that seemed too good to refuse. It was from an old friend, Marie — also a teacher — who told her that because her husband's job had been transferred to another town, she had to leave her part-time position at an Infants' School in Hildean, just two miles from our home. She wondered if Anita might be interested in the job. It entailed teaching the top infants' class on two afternoons every week. The last time Anita and Marie had met, they had both commented on what an ideal job hers was for a mother with a young family. Marie was sure that Miss Greenaway, the Headmistress, would appoint Anita on her recommendation.

Although she was attracted to the job, Anita thought it would not be possible to take it, as our three-year-old daughter had not yet started school. Marie passed on this information but Miss Greenaway did not see this as an insurmountable problem. So, a few days later, mother and child went in to meet the head.

"And how old is she?" enquired Miss Greenaway, smiling at our beautifully behaved daughter.

"Three."

Miss Greenaway wrote the figure "3" on a piece of paper and thoughtfully drew a circle around it. Then she looked up and smiled once more.

"She could join our reception class and spend the two afternoons there," she declared. "So that's the problem solved! Now, when are you able to start?"

Anita was back in Education!

Autumn term at Turnbrook Way was similar in many ways to the preceding Spring and Summer terms. Mr Handforth was at his desk for the first few mornings in September, but within a week his pattern of absences had returned. I was discouraged by this turn of events as the work-load during the Autumn term is always heavy. As Christmas approached, the staff became involved in practising carols and songs for the Carol Concert, organising Christmas parties, and bedecking the school with festive friezes, strings of paper chains and coloured lanterns.

My dilemma was that when Mr Handforth came into school he would take over all the arrangements — often reorganising plans that had already been made in his absence — and then go missing again for several days, unable to deal with resultant queries. In my deputy role, I was constantly frustrated, as I alternated between having total responsibility, and being completely disempowered.

As the weather worsened, Mr Handforth's health worsened too. His absences grew longer and inevitably some situations arose on which I needed his advice. On one such occasion I tentatively rang him at home from where he readily gave his opinion, advising me to telephone him whenever I met up with a problem. From then on this became the pattern of our communication as I came against new challenges. Whenever I spoke to him on the phone his breathlessness was all too apparent, but he strove to give the impression that this was only a temporary set-back and that he would soon be fighting fit and back to normal.

After Christmas, the weather was severe and the Head did not appear in school at all. I discovered that his home was quite close to the school and my telephone calls were eventually replaced by home visits. Once or twice a week, I would walk the quarter of a mile to his house to be let in by Mrs Handforth who would lead me into the front room to find a pale, diminutive figure wrapped in a blanket, hunched in an armchair. We would talk for a while, and I would pass on the latest information about school happenings. Then he would give me instructions on how to deal with particular situations.

Once or twice, I was shown upstairs to the bedroom where the Head lay propped up on pillows trying to appear as normal as possible. We conversed for a while, and he maintained his illusion of being in total charge of the school as he gave directives on routine administrative tasks and arrangements he wanted to be put into place. Although I saw that Mr Handforth was frail, I did not appreciate the extent of his illness nor recognise what must soon be the outcome.

One morning, a few weeks later, the telephone rang as I walked into the school office. It was Mrs Handforth.

"I'm afraid Mr Handforth passed away last night," she said. "I thought I'd better let you know."

I was absolutely shaken. I do not know what I said in reply, but no doubt I offered my condolences. When I had recovered a little, I went to tell the sad news to the staff, some of whom had worked with Mr Handforth for many years. The children duly arrived and were ushered into their classrooms, and I began to inform the Authorities of events. I spoke to Mr Hallows, the Divisional Education Officer, who said he would come to school during the morning so that we could discuss matters. He arrived just before lunch and did his best to boost my confidence.

"The primary role of the Deputy Head," he said, "is to step into the breach in a situation like this and take on the role of Head Teacher until a new Head Teacher is appointed. This cannot be before September as there is insufficient time to advertise the post and hold interviews. I will give you all the help I can — I'm just at the other end of the phone, so do feel free to ring me at any time."

Whilst I was grateful for his support, I also knew that he was unlikely to have the solution to many of the basic, practical problems that arise in schools. His job was concerned with administration, policy-making and negotiations around the purchase of stock. He would be unable to give advice with regard to an infant child who had to be dragged into the classroom screaming every morning because he had taken a dislike to school, or a parent who complained to the Head that her son could not get on with his teacher because she was "always picking on him".

I returned home that night with very mixed feelings. I was disconcerted by the enormity of what lay ahead, yet at the same time stimulated at the prospect of running the school in my own way for several months. Who knows? — were I to make a good job of it, I might be in the running when the new Head was appointed.

The following days and weeks were eventful but often difficult. There was the funeral, of course, to which members of the educational establishment and Head Teachers from far and wide came to pay their respects. Then, during the following weeks I continued to receive telephone calls from people who, as yet unaware of the situation, would ask to speak to Mr Handforth in person. To them I had to break the news, and, where appropriate, to pass on his home address so that a personal letter of condolence could be sent to Mrs Handforth.

★ ★ ★

In retrospect, I realise that I should have asked for more initial help in getting to grips with the situation. Although a teacher had been appointed to release me from my responsibilities with Primary 4, I had difficulty in planning my time in the office. I didn't always recognise what was likely to crop up. Sometimes I was at a loss, not knowing what to do — then out of the blue I would be pressurized to complete essential tasks which could have been done at a more leisurely pace had I foreseen that they would arise.

When not sure of the way ahead, I would consult with experienced members of staff and often went along with their suggestions that "We usually do this", or "we sometimes do that", which of course was not taking on my planned "leading role" or striking out in a new direction!

One morning at playtime, several children came rushing into school and began hammering on my office door. I flung it open, with a reprimand ready on my lips, but somehow their demeanor made me sense that something was seriously wrong.

"It's Mr Wilson sir, he's fallen off the roof!"

I hurried out into the playground to find the elderly caretaker, with the duty teacher in attendance, lying on his back on the tarmac looking decidedly unwell. I phoned for an ambulance and alerted the teachers in the staffroom before returning to attend to Mr Wilson in the playground, and to find out how the accident had happened.

The explanation was simple. At playtimes, the older boys often played football, using piles of coats as goalposts and the playground walls as the touchline. Occasionally, the ball would be kicked on to the school roof, sometimes bouncing back down, but more often becoming stuck in the gullies or guttering. Usually, another ball was available — several boys brought one to school — but if all the balls ended up on the roof the game came to an abrupt end.

At this point, the frustrated children would seek out the caretaker and plead with him to "get the balls down" and, always willing to please, Mr Wilson would get out his ladder. On this occasion he had climbed up and was about to throw down the balls when the ladder had slipped sideways, and he had fallen heavily onto the tarmac.

The ambulance duly arrived and carried him off to hospital with a badly broken leg, which was to keep him away from school for many months. A temporary caretaker had to be appointed, less familiar with the job, giving rise to further problems.

I went to see Mr Wilson several times in hospital and at his home. I got to know him better during these visits and made it clear to him, (and later to the children at school), that any ball coming to rest on the school roof from then onwards was destined to stay there until the next school holiday!

In due course an advertisement for the headship of Turnbrook Way Primary appeared in the educational press. I sent off for an application form. As I completed it and worked on my letter of application, I felt hopeful. I had coped reasonably well in a traumatic situation and had brought the school through a difficult time. Nothing had actually gone wrong — indeed everything had functioned relatively normally.

When the short list was drawn up, I was pleased to find that I had been included. I knew that in a situation like the present one, most short-listing panels would include the acting head out of courtesy, but even so my hopes remained high.

The interviews were held one evening after school, and as I sat in the staff room waiting to be called in, it dawned on me that my lack of experience put me at a grave disadvantage. Most of the other candidates had been deputy heads for a number of years and two of them were already head teachers of smaller schools. In the event, my interview went reasonably well, and the panel expressed their appreciation of the work I had done during my acting headship, but when the educational advisor came out at the end of the evening it was to call in another candidate.

When he re-emerged, having accepted the post, we all shook his hand and congratulated him warmly. But whilst the other candidates were returning home with feelings of disappointment, mine were of apprehension. For I knew that when the next academic year began, the man whose hand I had just shaken would be the decision maker, whilst once again I would be the deputy.

CHAPTER
FOUR

A Student Again

Andrew Deakin was a tall, middle-aged man with mousey hair, a ready smile and a Yorkshire accent. He had an air of relaxed authority about him. Unlike many head teachers, who in those days came to school in pinstripe suits, Andrew wore a brown corduroy jacket, unpressed trousers and a checked shirt. His clothes were functional, but smartness was not his top priority.

He was already in school when I arrived on the first day of the autumn term in September 1972, and he invited me into his room.

"I'm sure we'll get on very well together, Rod," he said. "Tell me about the staff."

I was amazed that he had called me by my first name. Throughout my career, and even in college, everyone had always addressed each other formally. I had always been "Mr Broome" to other members of staff, and I had always addressed them using their surname. Calling a colleague by his Christian name seemed very strange indeed — almost unprofessional at the time.

I named each teacher in the school, giving a brief summary of their talents and abilities. When, moments later, the morning bell sounded, I went on my way to Primary 4 classroom to resume my role as a class teacher.

There was a staff meeting later in the day and everyone soon realised that Andrew Deakin's relaxed attitude did not mean that he was willing to accept the status quo. To begin with, he did not like the fact that the school assembly took place first thing in the morning.

"I think the children should come into class at 9 o'clock and begin work right away," he said. "Walking out into the hall straight after registration and then returning for lessons afterwards creates a double disturbance. I would like to have a morning assembly at 10.30a.m. — following which the children could go straight out to play."

I am not sure what the others thought of this idea, but it seemed highly unusual to me. During my whole career in teaching, in every school in which I had taught, assembly had always taken place as soon as the children came in. And yet there was no denying the logic of what he said — a lot of time *was* wasted as classes walked back and forth.

"Now can we talk about playtimes?" he continued. "What happens at the moment?"

On behalf of the staff, I described how a bell monitor, using the wall clock in the hall, rang a handbell in school to alert the staff when playtime was over. The teacher on yard duty, hearing the bell, would blow a whistle and all the children would form lines in the playground. Then, on the teacher's signal, they would walk in an orderly fashion into school, hang up their coats in the cloakroom and make their way to the classrooms.

Andrew Deakin looked thoughtful.

"You know, I'm not sure there's a need for all that," he said. "Let's try ringing the bell and allowing the children to walk in when they hear it. They don't need to be regimented in that way."

Glancing around the room, I could tell that several of my colleagues shared my fear that hoards of children would rush to the nearest doorway, causing accidents and injuries — but out of deference to his position, no one questioned the wisdom of the suggestion.

In the event, it is true to say that although the children came in more noisily and were less orderly than before as they moved about the school, no child was ever hurt in any way.

Over the following weeks, changes were made in several areas of school life. Morning Assemblies, formerly the head teacher's preserve, were now led by groups of children who would choose the song to sing and perhaps read out prayers or pieces of writing they had prepared in class. Even infants took part in this way, the class teacher taking charge but groups of young children holding up pictures or saying poems.

I was uncertain how to view these changes. In theory I was in favour of new ways of doing things, but part of me wanted to resist the apparent freedom given to the children, for the school appeared noisier and less orderly, and life was becoming more stressful for the staff. At times, it was hard not to perceive some of the changes as a lowering of standards.

Throughout those first weeks, Andrew did not ask my opinion about anything. Although he was very courteous and friendly towards me, he didn't discuss any of the alterations he was about to make in the school. Perhaps he saw me as reactionary and thought I would argue with him or obstruct his "vision" in some way — and he had no intention of letting that happen.

In a conversation around Christmas time, he brought up a subject that made me think.

"How long is it since you left college?" he asked.

"Oh . . . about 14 years I think. Why?"

"You might be due for a long course," he said. "You had a particularly difficult time last year, and if you apply for secondment now, the *powers-that-be* might view it quite sympathetically."

That evening, I talked the matter over with Anita. Local authorities released a number of teachers each year on full pay to allow them to complete a course of approved study at a college or university.

Anita was encouraging.

"You've got nothing to lose," she declared. "Just fill in an application form and see what happens."

I was less certain than she was, though. What would happen if I got on a course only to discover that I couldn't cope with it? I had never been confident about my academic ability. When, a few days later, Mr Hallows, the Divisional Education Officer, called at the school, I took the opportunity to mention it to him.

"There's absolutely no reason why you shouldn't apply," he said. "As Mr Deakin mentioned it to you, he'll obviously support your application — but you'll have to be quick. The deadline for sending in secondment applications is in about three week's time. If you miss that, you'll have to wait for another year."

I needed no further encouragement to begin scouring the educational press for suitable courses, seeking out those aimed at developing teaching skills to be used with slower learners.

I had always had a soft spot for those who did not find learning easy. As a child at school I had usually found memorizing lists of names, countries or dates difficult — yet this ability was the very quality which tended to earn high marks in examinations. On the other hand, I was highly competent at remembering *processes* or working out *ways of doing things* — making me good at art, woodwork and other practical tasks — but these tended to be less well regarded. They were not useful in passing most school tests!

Perhaps because of this, on becoming a teacher, I had developed a special interest in children who struggled with the curriculum. I had observed that whilst some children learned to read with very little effort, others who tried just as hard and had lots of extra help from staff found the whole process of deciphering words or adding up numbers to be a gruelling task.

So it is not surprising that in my search for interesting courses, I began to focus on those designed to help teachers understand and work more effectively with disadvantaged children.

One morning I came across an advertisement for a course leading to a Diploma in Compensatory Education at Didsbury Teacher's Training College in Manchester. It seemed to be exactly what I was looking for. It was designed to explore ways of helping those pupils performing significantly below expected levels in reading, mathematics, and other subjects, yet not poorly enough to require the intervention of special education services. What is more, it was being held at the college at which I had initially trained as a teacher — although its name had now been upgraded to the rather grander-sounding Didsbury College of Education.

With Anita's encouragement, I sent off to the college and the Local Authority for the required forms, completed them, and returned them to the appropriate departments within the week.

Soon I was called for interview at Didsbury and within days heard that I would be offered a place on the course, provided the Local Authority granted me secondment. A few weeks later, I received a letter from the Divisional Education Officer stating that I would be given a year's secondment conditional upon Didsbury College of Education accepting me as a suitable student. Both pieces of the jigsaw fitted together perfectly. I knew that in a few months' time I would be freed from classroom responsibilities to plan my future direction and to explore in detail the concept of Compensatory Education.

The final months of the school year sped by, and one Monday morning in September 1973, instead of taking the familiar route to Turnbrook Way, I drove southward to re-acquaint myself with Didsbury College. It had been 14 years since my carefree time there as a student, and when I arrived I discovered, to my dismay, that everything had changed. The fine stone building once housing the men's and women's accommodation, the principal's office and the social room had been converted into administration offices. The lawns, paths and trees I had viewed from my study bedroom window had been buried beneath multi-storey edifices of concrete and brick, and high-rise halls of residence filled the once wooded fields.

Suppressing my feelings of disappointment, I followed the directions I had been given, and found the first floor suite of rooms aptly labelled: The Compensatory Education Unit.

There were to be 13 of us on the course and, after we had each introduced ourselves to the group, we listened to an introductory talk on the nature of the course.

I was a student once again and enjoyed the whole experience immensely — the lectures, school visits, participation in arguments stimulated by our young sociology lecturer, and days spent at home writing essays, reading relevant books and carrying out research.

In retrospect, two things stand out in my memory. The first was a visit to see groundbreaking work being done in a deprived area of Liverpool by Eric Midwinter and his team, the second, an embarrassing episode resulting from my attempts to help Anita with an infant class project.

At that time, it was becoming increasingly clear that things were beginning to change in the educational world. Educationalists had become aware that the home environment had a strong influence on a child's school achievement. They had looked at deprived communities or neighbourhoods and recognised that many of them were served by rundown schools staffed by disillusioned teachers. And the parents of many children who were now failing in school had themselves underachieved when they were pupils.

In 1967, the Plowden Committee had produced its report: *Children and their Primary Schools*. It had asserted that:

"A school is not merely a teaching shop; it must transmit values and attitudes . . . The school sets out deliberately to devise the right environment for children, to allow them to be themselves and to develop in the way and at the pace appropriate to them . . . It tries to equalise opportunities and compensate for handicaps . . . It lays special stress on individual discovery, on first hand experience and on opportunities for creative work. It insists that knowledge does not fall into neatly separate compartments, and that work and play are not opposite but complementary."

Drab buildings, fierce discipline and formal instruction were no longer seen as acceptable. And so in the years following the Report, areas of poverty and social deprivation in towns and cities had become defined as Educational Priority Areas and were given extra funding and better staffing ratios than other more affluent localities. Attempts were being made to involve parents in the education of their children by helping them to understand what their children were doing and encouraging them to take an active part in the process.

When we visited the Midwinter project in Liverpool, I was both stunned and inspired by what I saw. Rather than discouraging or at best tolerating the presence of parents within the school, in Liverpool we found an active policy of parental involvement. As we walked through the classrooms, I was amazed to see formal rows of desks replaced by children clustered in groups around tables, often accompanied by mums or dads. The adults — several of whom were smoking — were helping the children to work out the answers to "sums" or discussing a piece of writing. Many of the adults were poorly dressed, but they looked relaxed in the situation, and the teachers moved amongst them, helping both children and parents alike when explanations were needed. There was a feeling of happy cooperation within the building.

In the playground, a group of dads and older pupils, along with a class teacher, were busily painting a large mural along one of the walls of the playground. The principle behind this was that the area's continual problem with graffiti would be overcome if the people from the area decorated and "owned" their own locality and "protected" it from those who would spoil it.

The Midwinter project was a melting pot of creative ideas. Education should no longer be only for children — it should be available to all. As a centre of the community, a school should be the place where courses would meet the needs of all age groups and all abilities — a cradle-to-grave service which would enhance the quality of everyone's daily life. And being local, the building would be a visible demonstration in bricks and mortar of the continuity and never-ending nature of education.

The visit to Liverpool had a profound effect on me and greatly widened my educational horizons. However, one hurdle was still to be faced. To complete my course, I had to undertake a piece of original research, and produce a dissertation of 20,000 words.

During the course, I had become interested in a piece of research which had been carried out in the USA. Two researchers had convinced teachers that by using specific tests they were able to identify children who were due to make huge leaps forward in their educational progress. In actuality they gave no tests and chose the "star" pupils at random, yet these selected children did indeed make significant progress during the year. The researchers attributed this to "teacher expectation" — the teachers had *expected* unusual progress from certain children, and because of this it had happened!

I wanted to try to do a similar experiment in a local school, and approached Miss Greenaway, Anita's headmistress, to see if I could observe the children in her Infant School. She was most enthusiastic and allowed me to spend a couple of hours in reception class once a week for several months. It was on one of these visits that Anita asked me to help her with a class project — leading to that embarrassing episode!

Anita and her class of six-year-olds had been studying shops and the kinds of things they sold. For the final session, Anita intended to take the class for a walk around the streets to see the shops at first hand before making a huge wall collage. In preparation for the final display, she asked me to photograph all the local shops as I left after my observation session.

Dutifully I drove around, stopping to snap the butcher's, the baker's and the candlestick maker's through the driver's window, after which I returned home to write up my observation results.

I had been busily writing for about an hour when there was a knock at the front door. I opened it and was confronted by two policemen.

They pointed to my car, parked on the drive.

"Is this your vehicle, sir?"

I nodded.

"Have you been driving around Hildean taking photographs this afternoon, sir?"

"Yes, I have."

"Including the post office?"

"Er . . . yes."

"And why would you be doing that, sir?"

The reason for their visit hit me in a flash. In recent months there had been a spate of raids on sub-post offices and just a few weeks before, a postmaster had been shot and injured.

I tried to explain that I had been taking photographs for my wife who worked at All Saints Infant School in Hildean and was teaching her children about shops, but the more I gabbled on the more unlikely my explanation appeared. The officers wrote down the name of the school and the name of the headmistress, and as they drove away, I had no doubt that they were going to check my "alibi".

Twenty minutes later, I received a call from a chuckling Miss Greenaway, who had found the constables' visit highly amusing. Apparently, the postmaster had seen me photographing his premises, taken down the number of my car and alerted the police.

From then on, my school visits brought a smile to everyone's lips, and I knew they were visualising me as a bank robber!

Weeks passed, and I was more than half way through my course. What was to be my next move? I didn't want to fall back into a rut. My horizons were wider, and I could see new possibilities ahead. I would have an additional qualification when I left Didsbury, and I had been acting head for several months just over a year ago. I considered the time had come for me to apply for headships of small primary schools.

Once again, I studied the pages of the educational press in the hope of finding something suitable.

CHAPTER
FIVE

The Sow's Ear

As I leafed through the pages of the *Times Educational Supplement* during May 1974, one thing soon became clear: There were very few vacancies for head teachers being advertised. There would be one or two each week, usually in the south of England — but nothing within travelling distance of Rochdale.

Then, one day, I found one that looked more hopeful. A head teacher was required for a one-form-entry primary school in Merringham on the outskirts of Manchester, and the successful candidate would be required to start as soon as possible. The next morning, I quickly drove into Merringham, but finding the school was more difficult than I had expected. I stopped for directions several times before locating it in a run-down quarter of the town.

It was a dismal, single-storey building constructed in the days of Queen Victoria from Accrington stock brick and surrounded by a tiny, walled playground next to a main road. The high windows no doubt let in plenty of light, but were set too high in the walls to allow a view into, or out of, the classrooms. The children's toilets were situated in a corner of the playground.

Despite its bleak appearance, I decided to ring the education office to request an application form, but on doing so received a surprise.

"Oh, you mean *that* St Marks!" declared the clerk, after several abortive attempts to identify the school, "Let me explain . . . *that* school is closing down soon. We've just taken it over and I *think* a replacement school is being built close by. Shall I still send you a form?"

As I said "Yes", I realised that the clerk knew as little about the school as I did. Neither of us knew where the new building was, and I decided I would have to make another journey of exploration if I wanted to find it.

I eventually discovered that the new St Mark's Primary School was being built on a large, open, grassed site behind the graveyard of St Mark's Church. It was a single storey building which, when I first saw it, was surrounded by trucks, piles of earth and workmen's cabins. It had been commissioned by a division of Lancashire County but when the new Metropolitan Boroughs were formed during 1974, it had been transferred to the local authority at Merringham within the Greater Metropolitan County of Manchester. This was the reason the clerk in "the office" knew so very little about it.

I wandered around the site, trying to assess how close it was to completion, and came upon a man carrying a clipboard.

"When will it be finished?" I asked.

He smiled and shook his head. "Your guess is as good as mine," he replied. "It's supposed to be opening in September, but the Local Authority at Merringham didn't even know it was here until a few weeks ago!"

In spite of the chaotic situation, I decided to apply for the headship. I was excited by the prospect of running a brand new school and conjectured that because of the mix-up, there might be fewer people applying for the job.

In retrospect, I realise I must have breezed through the interview, appearing confident and knowledgeable. I talked about my months as Acting Head at Turnbrook Way Primary and was able to discuss in detail the Plowden Report, compensatory education, parental involvement in schools, and the school as a centre of the community. The course at Didsbury had certainly made me *au fait* with all the modern developments in education and given me new confidence in my own leadership qualities.

I was offered the post and told that as they were hoping to open the new school at the beginning of the autumn term in September, I should send in my resignation to Lancashire Division 23 without delay.

I returned home in a state of high excitement.

"I knew you'd get it!" Anita exclaimed, throwing her arms around me. "Tell me all about the school. What is it like? Will you have to appoint new teachers?"

"I'm not really sure about anything," I confessed. "The building is only partly finished at the moment — it's just an outer shell really — but it *is* set in the middle of large grounds. Apparently there are going to be two football pitches. But I don't think I'll have to appoint staff — it's a *replacement* school. The teachers will be moving to the new building when it opens in September, and the old head teacher has decided to retire. All I need to do at the moment is hand in my notice."

But when I did so, I was in for a shock. It was early June, and I had missed the final date for summer resignations by a couple of weeks. Usually local authorities would be flexible in such cases, allowing a teacher to leave as long as a replacement could be found, but Lancashire Division 23 dug their heels in. They decided to hold me to my contract, which meant that I would not be able to take up my post at the new school until January 1975. The clipboard man's joke that the Education Department at Merringham "did not know the school was there" had more than a grain of truth in it — they had not advertised the headship post early enough. For me, this would mean that although I had a new job, I was forced to return to Turnbrook Way as deputy head for one more term. For the new St Marks, it meant that the school was destined to open with a newly appointed head who was unable to take up his post!

I attended Didsbury for the rest of the academic year, took my examinations and gained my diploma, but my mind was focused on the new school at Merringham. I visited the site at regular intervals to see how the building was progressing. By the time the summer holiday arrived the external structure was finished and most of the internal fittings had been completed, but it was still far from habitable. The carpets had not been laid and almost no furniture had been delivered to the school.

On one visit, I noticed something unusual about the layout of the school building. When I had applied for the job, I had realised that the school was "open plan" in design, and that instead of having separate classrooms with doors, the children would be assigned to various open areas within the building. But as I walked around inside the school, it dawned on me that the new St Marks had only *five* of these bays. How were three infant classes and four junior classes meant to fit into five work bays?

I took the first opportunity to meet with the schools commissioning officer and we studied the architect's plan together.

"Ah, I can explain that," he said, when I asked him about the two missing bays. "It had already been decided when the school was handed over to Merringham that the anticipated number of pupils would not warrant a full one-form entry school, so the planners made the building smaller."

He pointed to the plan, and I could see that two junior work bays and a section marked "School Library" had been crossed out. About a fifth of the school had just not been built — and what remained was totally unbalanced in terms of the ages of children it had to accommodate!

I studied the drawing more closely.

"Where are the cloakrooms?" I asked. In every school in which I had ever worked there had been cloakrooms with washbasins. In Turnbrook Way Primary there were two — one for infants and one for juniors. I was unable to find a single cloakroom on this plan.

"Oh there aren't any cloakrooms," declared the commissioning officer. "We supply trolleys."

"*Trolleys?*"

The commissioning officer could tell by my tone of voice that he had some explaining to do.

"It's nothing to do with me," he protested. "It's all about saving money. You see, every child is allocated a certain number of square feet of 'teaching space', so you decide on the number of children to be housed, multiply it by so many square feet, and — *hey presto!* — you have the size of the building. Of course, you have to add on the head's room, the staff room, the school kitchen, the caretaker's room and the toilets — all non-teaching areas — but children's cloakrooms or washrooms would count as *additional* non-teaching space, so instead they supply trolleys for coats."

"Which is why there are rows of tiny sinks against some of the walls instead of washrooms," I said, beginning to understand.

He nodded. "They're all included in the 'teaching space'," he replied.

I looked at the plan again and realised that there were no corridors, entrance halls or reception areas. One could not move from place to place within the building without walking through teaching areas where

49

pupils and teachers would be engaged in lessons! No doubt the architects had been told to design a school which would be open and welcoming to parents — but workmen, delivery men, salesmen, health visitors, nurses and attendance officers also visit schools, and all would walk through teaching areas whenever they came into the building.

It was becoming increasingly obvious that I would have the unenviable task of making a silk purse out of a sow's ear.

A few days later, I visited the old St Marks building to meet the staff. On arrival, I was welcomed by the head, and it became evident that although he was close to retiring age, he had made the decision to leave early rather than face the upheaval of moving to the new school.

The Victorian building was indeed old and in bad repair, but I could see that there was a lot more space available than in the new school. A high, central assembly hall with a stage at one end was flanked on all sides by generously-sized classrooms, divided from each other by wood and glass partitions, and there was ample room to move from place to place along corridors lined with white tilefaced bricks. Close to the children's entrance, I could see a large alcove containing the familiar metal framework which supported rows of children's coat hooks, and there was a line of good-sized, but old-fashioned washbasins along one of the walls.

The staff of five teachers and one nursery assistant was extremely apprehensive — and indignant — about their move to the new school. They deeply resented being thrust into a new, open-plan building with less space and, to them, poorer facilities. They had had no training in the "new" methods of education and seemed determined to maintain the "*status quo*". The deputy head, Mr Heggarty, had been "emergency trained" after the war and was also approaching retirement age. He was a short, white-haired man with a gentle personality, but one of the "old school" who was used to formal methods and tight discipline. I was not sure how he would take to working in an open plan school under the leadership of a much younger man.

As the Autumn term began, I realised that it was going to be a difficult one. The Merringham Education Department had appointed the deputy head of a large, local primary school to be Acting Head of St Marks until I was able to take up my post after Christmas. She had been a business executive before becoming a teacher in her mid-thirties, and had a reputation for being decisive and dynamic. The exact opposite of what I thought was needed to ease apprehensive and vulnerable teachers into a new regime.

I made a commitment to visit the school whenever I could during that first term, although as I had a class to teach at Turnbrook Way, this was far from easy. Fortunately, Andrew Deakin was very understanding and demanded little of me in my role as his deputy, so two or three times a week during my lunch break and

every day after school I would drive over to St Marks —
a journey of several miles — to check up on the
situation there.

Things were not going smoothly. In order to help
matters, I had arranged for the children to be admitted
a few at a time over the first week of term. But in spite
of superhuman efforts by the teachers, each day seemed
to be filled with a new crisis. Some of the new furniture
was still undelivered, and the large, worn cupboards
that had been brought from the old school looked
incongruous in the new, bright, smaller building and
took up too much space. In addition, workmen were
arriving daily to finish off some half-completed task —
laying a piece of carpet, fixing a loose door handle, or
mending a leaking tap — and delivery men were
continually staggering through the class areas with
storage cupboards or shelving units, asking, "Where do
you want this?" They interrupted lessons, already
proving difficult for the teachers because of new
surroundings and unfamiliar teaching methods.

I was as positive and supportive as I could be, but I
knew that after Christmas, there would be much to sort
out.

CHAPTER
SIX

A New Way of Doing Things

The new St Marks C.E. Primary School was unlike any other school in the surrounding district. It was fully open-plan in design. The staff room, the head's room and the caretaker's room were enclosed, but only two other rooms in the building had doors. The first was marked "audio visual room" on the plan and was in the centre of the building. It was designed to show films or television programmes and could be used for the storage of valuable electrical equipment. The second room, which was little bigger than a domestic bathroom, had an internal glass window for supervision purposes. It was marked "study area" on the plan.

The remainder of the building was made up of five carpeted work bays which were linked together by "wet areas" (with sinks), "craft areas" (with vinyl floor tiles), or "reading and study areas", (with soft furnishings and carpets). There was a small outside play area for reception children that was sheltered to some extent by a polycarbonate roof but remained open to the elements along one side.

Most of the interior walls of the building (which had been left as unpainted breeze block) were covered by broad strips of coloured pin-board stretching from floor to ceiling. Chalk boards had not been supplied, as they did not fit in with the "new" methods, but with great foresight the teachers had brought one or two blackboards and easels from the old building.

There were four small stockrooms, each about the size of a domestic toilet. In order to keep non-teaching space to a minimum, the planners had made three of these double as the location for a large cold water storage tank. Hence the back third of each stockroom could only be reached by almost kneeling down and crawling under the tank. In addition, the limited width of the rooms meant that large sheets of art paper could not be stored satisfactorily.

In the old school, each child had an individual desk with a lift-up lid for storage. These were now replaced by tables, and children were supplied with personal storage trays in which to put their pencils, rulers and exercise books. They were kept in a special unit at one side of the class area, or "Homebase", as it came to be called. This meant that whenever an activity was changed, there was mass movement to and from the storage units to get out or put away equipment.

Two further innovations were doors that led directly out of each class area into the playground, and floor-to-ceiling windows letting in maximum light.

Initially we thought these doors would be very convenient but their positioning meant that on wet days children walked straight into their Homebases from outside, thus soiling the carpets with their dirty shoes and wet coats, and on cold days the open door drained all the heat from the teaching area.

Although the floor-to-ceiling windows let in plenty of light, there were disadvantages here too. Quite often, at 9 o'clock in the morning as children came in, or just before home time in the afternoon, groups of parents or grandparents would stand outside the windows peering at the children inside — sometimes waving or mouthing messages through the glass which was a distraction for both children and teachers.

There was also the problem of the trolleys. For generations, young children had been taught to find their outdoor coats at playtimes and home time by knowing their peg's position in the cloakroom and looking for their special picture on the peg. Now we had coat trolleys on castors which, on being moved, could easily be reversed. This meant that a child's coat could no longer be found by "position". Many times a week a tearful infant would go to a teacher saying his or her coat had disappeared when they were merely looking on the wrong side of the trolley. Planners never seem to foresee problems like this!

My staff, having moved into the new St Marks School from an old Victorian building, were finding the adjustment difficult and distracting, and suddenly their job seemed very much harder.

However, changes were being introduced that covered far more than the physical structure of school buildings. Those at school in the 1940s or 50s will recall sitting in pairs at double desks facing the front of the class. The teacher — chalk in hand — would give instruction on some point in mathematics or English, or perhaps ask a child to stand and read aloud from the class text book. Inability to live up to what was expected could result in ridicule, or at worst, punishment. By the 60's, the most oppressive regimes were coming to an end, but the teacher was still to be found at the front of the class bestowing knowledge to every listening child as they studied the same page in a book or the same piece of writing on the blackboard.

Of course, this way of teaching took no account of individual abilities in pupils — the fact that some were brighter than others — and there was little attempt to stimulate the pupils so that they would actually *want* to learn. Sometimes lessons contained difficult ideas which were hard to comprehend, so facts were chanted by rote until they could be "parroted" back to prove that they had been learnt. Is it any wonder that many children hated school and couldn't wait to leave?

In the 1960's, the Plowden Report was published, and people began to question whether the "old ways" were bringing out the best in children. A new philosophy was born — *child-centred education* — which recognised the child as an individual with unique qualities and abilities waiting to be developed.

In response to this new way of thinking, architects and planners began to design buildings which were bright and cheerful, based on the idea that children would be taught individually or in small groups. The belief was that pupils would be so motivated by the stimulating environment around them that they would long to discover things for themselves — with little or no supervision from teachers.

When I finally moved to St Marks in January 1975, the staff was severely stressed, struggling to cope with a different way of teaching in a new and alien environment.

They felt they had no privacy. Whereas in the old St Marks School their mistakes or inadequacies could go unnoticed, in the new environment, where teachers could see (and often hear) each other working, embarrassing situations or moments of indiscipline could be overheard by all. Several parents, who had volunteered to help in the new school, could also see the teachers in action and perhaps judge their performance.

It was a problem too that children were not always under the eye of their teacher. A group of children might be working in an adjoining "wet" area, perhaps filling a variety of containers with water to find out which had the greatest capacity. It took trust to allow them to work out of one's sight. What would happen if the children *did* begin to misbehave? Was it acceptable for another teacher to step in and correct them? Teachers were not used to other members of staff "interfering" with their class — it just wasn't done!

Mr Heggarty, the deputy head, had planned his own way of dealing with the move. He had brought with him from the old school a number of tall cupboards which he placed strategically around his Homebase, virtually

57

shutting himself in and forming his own "classroom". Within this area he arranged the plastic-topped tables in rows, put a backboard at the front, and tried — as near as possible — to reproduce the same conditions as in the building he had just left. However, the new Homebases were considerably smaller than the old classrooms, as it was not intended that children should remain in them all day, so the result was that within the area he had created there was barely room to move!

I empathized with Mr Heggarty. In the old school, his class of ten-year-olds had become accustomed to strict rules and procedures — including tight discipline — and now, all at once, they were expected to be mature and behave well with minimum supervision. No one had prepared them for the move or trained them to work in a responsible way, so some would misbehave when they were not under his direct supervision.

There was deep resentment throughout the staff. They had not been prepared for this transfer to a different form of education. They had had no special training or even the opportunity to spend time in other open-plan schools. Now they were having to learn "on the job" under the critical eye of colleagues, visitors and parents.

I was in a difficult position. Although I could understand the staff's aggrieved feelings, I had been appointed to lead, and make a success of, this new, modern school with its "forward-looking" educational system.

My task was to build up confidence and change perceptions. I decided to focus on three areas:

- Gaining the confidence of the parents
- Building up staff morale and self-belief
- Getting down to some physical work — with hammer and nails!

In the same way that the staff and children were unprepared for the move, so were the parents. They were at a loss to know what to make of the new building! As they stared through the windows, it seemed to them that the children were just "playing". And play — they thought — was not *learning*! I needed to find a way in which to explain what we were doing. I knew that some private schools issued brochures so I decided to produce one for St Marks. My resources were limited as the only reprographic equipment we had in school was a standard typewriter and a spirit duplicator — but, using my creativity and artistic abilities, I designed an attractive front cover bearing the title: They Don't Just Play All Day.

Inside, I explained the workings of small groups; how children were given practical tasks and recorded their results, thus learning facts and methods almost without realising they were doing so.

I explained that the Reading Centre I had set up in the small "study area" within the school contained hundreds of books drawn from different reading schemes with differing teaching approaches. This allowed children to be given the right material, enabling

59

them to progress at their optimum speed in reading and language.

My final stroke was to invite the parents to come into school at any time to ask questions or to see what their children were doing — and even join in with the lessons if they wanted to.

Of course this was a revolutionary step at a time when the teachers already felt threatened and vulnerable. During staffroom breaks they often complained about parents staring in through windows or, if the parents were in school, that they listened with avid attention to everything being said to the children.

"It's like teaching in a goldfish bowl!" they would mutter resentfully.

Although I recognized that such close scrutiny could be intimidating, I tried to promote a more positive view of the situation. I used phrases such as "We're all in this together", "We've got nothing to hide" and "We are a cooperative team with joint responsibilities", in the hope of modifying attitudes and lessening fears. Over the next few months, teacher-confidence did improve, and we all became far more relaxed about working in the public arena.

The final area for action required a lot of thought and some "elbow grease" on my part. The omission of two junior work-bays and a school library had left the physical provision for older children seriously depleted. They had less space than they needed and, as a library was essential, one had to be re-created in the entrance foyer. This was not very convenient as it was a long way from the class Homebases.

The coat trolleys on castors were proving to be a thorough nuisance. They took up a great deal of space, caused the constant problem of "missing" coats, and afforded an ideal hiding place or even a mode of transport for mischievous children! Using some of the school allowance, I bought long lengths of veneered chipboard, mounted them along the interior walls of the school and screwed onto them rows of aluminium coat hooks. It was by no means an ideal solution, but infinitely better than the previous arrangement.

Then there was the problem of the tiny stockrooms. Although suitable for storing exercise paper or packs of exercise books, they could not hold equipment or large sheets of drawing paper or card. I decided to build a new stockroom within a suitable alcove and, with the help of the caretaker, constructed a wooden frame and clad it with plasterboard. Inside we fixed broad shelves and allowed plenty of room for access. A final coat of paint and a locking door completed the job, much to everyone's relief.

As time passed, things became easier. Most teachers grew accustomed to working in an open environment, and as new children were admitted into Reception Class, we trained them in our way of working and encouraged them to behave responsibly even when out of sight.

CHAPTER
SEVEN

Pros and Cons

Throughout this turbulent time in my professional career, Anita was at home playing the calming and supportive role of "a listening ear". With her I could relax and enjoy being with our children — and frequently grumble about the latest ridiculous situation that had arisen at school! Anita showed patience and understanding, but at times she must have felt like shutting me in a cupboard!

Her teaching time had been increasing at All Saints. First it was one extra half-day a week, and then another, until by the mid 1970s she had a permanent part-time contract for 2½ days a week. It was ironic that she had trained at College to teach secondary science and now found herself teaching music to 5 and 6 year olds — and she loved it!

Although Anita was an accomplished pianist, she knew that very young children learn music best by singing along with an adult who is sitting amongst them as part of their group. So she spent much of each music lesson singing nursery rhymes, "action" songs, limericks, calypsos, musical story rhymes, and English folk songs — and before long every infant class in the school had a wide repertoire of musical items which they delighted in singing to anyone willing to listen.

But, as our own children grew older, Anita felt the need of a fresh challenge. For many years her time had been taken up with domestic tasks and the unavoidable "taxi" duties which emerged as our children played instruments, joined dancing classes and became members of youth groups.

In 1975, Anita decided to do something for herself. She applied for a place on the Open University Arts Foundation Course. It was a perfect choice! She found the text books and television broadcasts enthralling as they presented new concepts and widened her horizons. At the weekly seminars at Rochdale College, she met fellow students, who shared her enthusiasm for art, philosophy, music and literature. During the summer of 1976, she attended a summer school at York University. It was the perfect finale to a most enjoyable year.

By contrast, her second year proved to be a disaster. The academic workload doubled and Anita discovered her choice of course to be less interesting. There were fewer tutorials, so the students did not build up the same quality of rapport as in the first year. For several months she soldiered on, but the vital spark of enthusiasm had faded. Interaction with other students had provided the stimulus; alone with text books and television, her interest had waned. Regretfully, she withdrew from the course.

* * *

Halfway through the first year at the new St Marks, Mr Heggarty told me that, although still a year or so short of retirement age, he intended to finish at the end of the summer term.

Although he would have no pension until he reached his sixty-fifth birthday, he knew that after a lifetime of traditional teaching, he would be unable to adapt to the new educational methods. I felt sorry for his situation, but not surprised. He had been having difficulty in keeping his class in order, and the children, aware of his struggles with the new building, had made the most of the situation.

The Deputy Headship post was duly advertised and eventually a local man from a nearby school was appointed. He interviewed well and came with a high recommendation from his boss. I took to him immediately. Terry Jones was highly competent, practical, and very conscientious, and was to remain my deputy head until I retired.

Another change at that time was the appointment of a new vicar at St Mark's Church. This had a positive effect on the school as the vicar of the church was always, by tradition, the Chairman of the School Managers. The Reverend Charles Strong had been called into the ministry in middle age, having spent several years in industry, so he was a practical man with lots of common sense. From the first, he showed interest in the staff and the day-to-day workings of the school and, after a year or two, volunteered to take morning assembly every Wednesday morning.

★ ★ ★

Soon after taking up my job, I was visited by our educational advisor, Harold Arkwright, himself a former primary head, who was interested in the new methods being introduced. After several visits, he said that he was impressed by the organisation and relaxed atmosphere within the school. He thought the Reading Centre, with its readily available supply of books, was a good idea, and he appreciated the "thematic approach" we were developing. A class teacher would choose a theme considered of interest to her children, and for several weeks most lessons would revolve around that subject.

For example, during the summer term "Holidays at the Seaside" might be the topic, and lessons in mathematics, English, history, geography, science, nature study, art and craft, etc. would be woven around the theme. The climax to the topic often involved an educational visit, in this case maybe to a seaside town. Such an approach stimulated a lively interest in the subject, and children would bring in photographs, magazine articles or objects relating to the theme, which would then be used in a class display.

One morning, Harold Arkwright made a special request: Would I be willing to give a lecture to a group of local heads on the ways I had organised the school and on our educational methods? Pausing for only a moment, I declined the invitation. Although confident in planning educational programmes and implementing schemes of work, I felt unable to stand up and speak about them in public. As a result, I missed an opportunity for self promotion which was later to be taken up by several of my contemporaries, who had "captured the vision" further down the line. In subsequent years, I attended any number of lectures in which a confident speaker sought to inspire the audience with the very educational methods and innovations I had been using for years.

However, teachers from neighbouring schools were always made welcome whilst we were in session. Perhaps once or twice a week, two or three teachers would arrive at my office door. After I had explained our philosophy and methods to them, they were free to walk around the building observing the children and asking members of staff a variety of questions. After a while the class teachers began to enjoy the experience of being seen as innovators, admired and respected for their special abilities. However, not all visiting teachers were won over, and one or two left muttering, "Well, *I* could never work in that way!"

Despite the increasing confidence of the staff, there were certain ongoing disadvantages of working at St Marks. It was undoubtedly more stressful teaching in an open plan building than in a conventional school, and there were virtually no occasions when a member of staff could decide to "take it easy" for a day.

For example, if a teacher in a conventional school awoke feeling unwell one morning, she might decide to go to work and sit quietly at her desk for most of the day, having given the children some time-consuming exercises to complete. Whilst this was not ideal, it did mean that the children were contained within their own classroom, disrupting no other lessons. However, in an open plan school, such a teacher would know she was not well enough to teach groups of active, enquiring children and would therefore ring in sick.

This created a difficult situation for the rest of the staff. Sometimes, I was free to step into the breach for a day or half a day, but often I had engagements in my diary which could not be changed. So inevitably, the children had to be shared out between the other classes and were given work to do that was not relevant to their current "theme". This made discipline more difficult to maintain.

A further disruption to school life was caused by regular attacks of vandalism. St Marks' floor-to-ceiling windows, once broken, gave easy access to the inside of the school with little danger to the intruders.

The first break-in happened when we had been open for only a few weeks. The school had no alarm system, so the problem lay undiscovered until Joe Jackson, the caretaker, arrived for work at 8 o'clock the following morning. His immediate priorities were to pick up all the fragments of glass scattered widely over the carpeted area — a major hazard for small children — and to board up the broken window to conserve any remaining heat.

From that time on, we had break-ins every few weeks, and Mr Jackson constantly repeated the same procedure. Our all-time low was 13 forced entries in one year — a depressing state of affairs. And we were soon to discover another disadvantage of our floor-to-ceiling windows! They came down to ground level and safety regulations stated that the bottom pane of each window, which was a metre high, had to be made of toughened glass to prevent injury in the case of accidental breakage. These panes proved very difficult to replace. Each piece of glass had to be ordered and specially manufactured, so it was often a month or two before a workman came to replace it. In the meantime, we were patched up with random boards fitted in frames around the lower part of the building, which in no way enhanced its beauty!

The design of the roof became another source of problems. It was basically a felt-covered, flat roof, but over its entire area it had undulations, gentle slopes, gullies and peaks. Local youths quickly identified it as an ideal skateboarding rink — even though it was 14 feet or more above ground level! We had early reports of teenagers zooming back and forth across the roof on skateboards, performing various leaps and acrobatic manoeuvres and generally enjoying themselves. On occasions, youths were even spotted doing "wheelies" on mountain bikes! Joe Jackson went back to school in the evening on several occasions, but his attempts to persuade the lads to come down were met with laughter and derision. When he appealed to the police they were reluctant to respond to what they considered an "unimportant" issue.

After a while, during heavy rain storms, the inevitable leaks began to appear throughout the building. The wheels of the skateboards and the heel-plates on the boys' shoes had punctured the felt, allowing water to leak into the building. Patch-up repairs never lasted for very long, and the problem was only cured, several years later, when a complete re-felting of the roof was undertaken using a tough, high tensile felt, several times stronger (and much more expensive) than ordinary felt.

And so the years passed. Children were admitted, progressed through the school, and moved on to secondary education. Teachers came and went — but 3 members of staff remained, sharing with me the highs and lows, and possessing a wealth of experience to pass on to new members of staff as they were appointed.

Terry Jones, the deputy head, was an ideal "sounding board", against whom I could bounce ideas and be sure of a balanced response; Janet Clarke, who had worked at St Marks — old and new — since qualifying 20 years earlier was reliable and trustworthy; and Cathy Green, our Reception Class teacher, had a gentle manner which enabled new entrants to feel secure and established in them good behaviour patterns and sound work habits.

Mrs Mullen, the school clerk, and Mr Jackson, the school caretaker, were also long-established members of staff, providing stability and knowledge in administrative and maintenance matters.

All were still employed at the school in the academic year 1984–1985, the year in which I made a life-changing decision.

PART TWO

CHAPTER
EIGHT

Ten Years On

Autumn 1984 was St Mark's anniversary — it was exactly 10 years since the traumatic opening of the school. On the first day of the new term, my mind went back to those distant days, and the chaos that had reigned during the early weeks of September 1974. Thank goodness things were more settled now!

All our current pupils had been admitted at 4 years old and had grown up within our open plan environment. They knew the layout of the building. They got on with their work even when their teacher was occupied with another group; they asked for anything they needed in a polite manner; and they rarely caused a disturbance as they moved through different areas around the school.

By now, we had a band of willing parents who came in to help on a regular basis. They listened to children read or assisted with practical maths or craft activities. And Reverend Strong, Chairman of the School Managers (later to be called Governors), called in at least once a week to catch up on school matters and join the staff for a cup of coffee at playtime.

★   ★   ★

I was looking forward to this academic year — it could prove to be refreshingly different! For one thing, there were three new members of staff to welcome.

Deputy Terry Jones had been granted a year's secondment to take a B.Ed degree course, and his replacement as acting deputy head, was to be Vincent Leach. Vincent had taught in the Authority for a number of years and was hoping to gain further experience to help his future career.

Lesley Dunn had been appointed to replace a teacher who had moved on. She had been teaching Middle School children for several years, but had applied for our vacancy in order to return to her first love — the junior child.

I had interviewed Sally Ward under a different name before the holiday, but she had returned to take up her post two months later with her brand new married name. She was a fully trained infant teacher but had been appointed on a part-time job-share basis. She was to be the class teacher of Primary 2 every morning, whilst Janet Clarke, our longest serving member of staff, would take the reins every afternoon.

I put down my briefcase, hung up my coat and went on a tour of the building. Rounding a corner, I saw the caretaker peering shortsightedly at a large can of floor polish.

"Good morning, Joe. How's things? Er . . . anything wrong?"

Joe looked above the glasses perched on the end of his nose.

"It's not as good as it used to be," he said, nodding towards the can. "Here, come and look at this."

I followed him to the school hall where he pointed to the large expanse of parquet floor which was gleaming like a mirror under several new coats of polish.

"It looks perfect to me, Joe," I said.

"Ah, but you wait until after assembly when all the children have been in," he grumbled. "You'll see every scuff mark!"

I left Joe shaking his head despondently and was on my way to see if Vincent had arrived when I met Mrs Mullen coming into school. She didn't usually work on Thursday mornings, but as this was the first day of term she had come in to collect and bag up the children's dinner money ready for me to take to the bank. We exchanged greetings, and she went into the small office that had been installed just inside the front door of the school. For her first few years in the building, Mrs Mullen's "office" had been a melamine-topped table in a corner of the staffroom!

I found Vincent in his Homebase shuffling through some papers on his desk. He was obviously preoccupied, so after a quick "Good morning!" I went along to Homebase 1 where I found Cathy Green peering into a large, newly-opened cardboard box.

"It's our new computer — it's just been delivered," she said. "Do you think I should try to set it up this morning?"

75

"Rather you than me," I replied. "At least you have had some experience in dealing with computers."

Cathy pulled a face. She had been on the Authority's computer familiarisation course, so how ever little she knew, it would be more than the rest of us. Fortunately the new Reception children were not going to be admitted for a couple of days so she would be free to put her knowledge to the test.

The school kitchen, working under a temporary cook-supervisor, was a hive of activity. Before the holiday, I had sat in on an interview to appoint a new cook-supervisor. Derek Broadbent — *a man!* — had been chosen, and in a conversation later he said that he wished to be addressed as "Chef". I suspected that that would create a stir in the kitchen when he took up his duties in a few days time!

Before the morning bell rang, I fitted in a brief word with the remaining members of staff: Diane Davies, nursery assistant in Primary 1, and Hilary Varley, employed on a temporary contract to teach Primary 3 children during the maternity leave of their regular teacher.

The monitor arrived to ring the morning bell as I walked into my room, and moments later the children filed into school and the new school year had begun.

As soon as we had eaten lunch, I held a brief staff meeting designed to welcome the new teachers as part of the team. I stressed that although working in our open-plan building meant that mistakes could be seen by all, the plus side was that there were always others around to help out and give a hand when needed.

The meeting lasted only a few minutes, after which everyone gathered around Cathy who had arranged all the parts of our new computer on a trolley and was busily connecting everything together with masses of wires.

"The Local Authority has sent a computer to each of its schools," I said, "so I suppose we'll have to learn how to use it. In fact," I joked, "I think it is the duty of all teachers under the age of 46 to become competent at using computers in education!"

Vincent grinned across at me and immediately lowered the upper age-limit to 40. The afternoon bell sounded and the smiling staff returned to their classes for the afternoon session.

Within a week everyone had settled into the familiar routine, and I had admitted two new pupils. I was visited by a member of St Marks Church who reminded me that the church would be celebrating its centenary in 1985. He wondered if we had any material or information about the "new school" that he could include in a booklet he was preparing to mark the occasion.

"When was this building actually opened?" he asked, "and does it have a foundation stone?"

Without mentioning the catastrophic state of affairs in 1974, I explained that the school had never been officially "opened" and had no foundation stone.

"However," I added, "I do have *something* here that might interest you."

Going to my filing cabinet, I took out two very old school log books, filled with entries in copperplate handwriting from the previous century. They contained numerous accounts of poverty and sickness, of children being unable to attend school because they had no shoes, and reports from visiting inspectors whose primary task was to test the pupils on their knowledge of the Bible. The previous head had passed them on to me before he retired. I agreed to lend them to my visitor for his research.

He was highly delighted, and told me that the actual date of the centennial anniversary was 2nd February 1985, when a special service would be held in church, followed by a Social in the evening. The school was to be invited to take part in the celebrations. I made a note to mention it to the staff, particularly Janet Clarke, our music specialist, so that we could think about a possible contribution.

A few days later, I called a meeting to fix the date of our Harvest Festival Service. This, as usual, would be held in the school hall on a morning in October, and parents and relatives would be invited to join us. Each class would present an item, perhaps a poem or a short play, or — in the case of the four year olds — simply hold up an "Autumn picture". Items would be interspersed with familiar hymns joyously sung by everyone. In recent years the service had been led by

Reverend Strong, and I felt confident that he would be willing to take part again.

Earlier in the day, I had asked Cathy Green if, at the end of the meeting, she would give a short demonstration of our new BBC Acorn computer and explain some basic facts. Now she plugged in the computer and began to load a programme.

Everyone in the room became fascinated by the colourful displays and the electronic beeps coming from the monitor, and deeply interested in Cathy's activities. She was inundated by streams of questions flowing from the staff. Then each teacher in turn, under Cathy's direction, began to operate the keys and work through the educational programme that Cathy had loaded up. An early comment was, "I didn't realise you had to be able to type to use one of these." We were all engrossed by the keys being pressed and the computer's response.

Our exercise was brought to an abrupt halt by the afternoon bell, and everyone hurried off to their class to begin the afternoon's work.

By 1984, Anita's circumstances had changed, too. The number of children on roll at All Saints Infant School had fallen over successive years and by the end of the 70's the school was deemed to be over staffed. Although Anita's permanent part-time contract meant that her employment could not be terminated, she had to agree to be redeployed to a different school where there was a vacancy.

She was transferred to St Ambrose Primary School in Merringham, where once again she taught infants and specialised in music. When she first joined the school she was based in an annex well away from the main body of the school and worked alongside two elderly, very traditional women teachers. They had been colleagues for many years in their remote outpost, and seemed to resent Anita's relative youth and enthusiasm. They knew each other well, but still addressed each other formally, using title and surname. Anita's first *faux pas* had been to introduce herself with the words, "Hello, my name is Anita."

Gradually however, she had won them over with her pleasant manner and sound teaching abilities and within a year or two she had become firm friends with one of the ladies — Mrs Watson — who, like us, lived in Rochdale. The strange thing was that in spite of their developing friendship, for many months Mary Watson insisted on addressing Anita as "Mrs Broome", whereas whenever *my* name came up in the conversation, she would refer to me as "Rod"!

One day Mary invited us both to her home for supper so that we could meet her husband, but Anita told me that before accepting the invitation she had laid down a condition. "I said I couldn't possibly accept if she continued to call me 'Mrs Broome' and address you as 'Rod'!"

That did the trick! Mary at first looked bewildered but then chuckled in surrender. A close friendship was established between them which lasted until Mary died fifteen years after her retirement. In fact, Mary Watson actually began to call Anita by her Christian name at school, although occasionally she would be overheard mentioning "Mrs Broome" and "Rod" in the same sentence when speaking to others!

Soon after the beginning of the Autumn Term, Anita came home with some surprising news about one of St Marks' neighbouring schools.

"Have you heard about Beech Street?" she asked, "Surveyors have declared it structurally unsound. The Authority is deciding between carrying out massive repairs, or demolishing it and building a new school."

"How do you know that? Beech Street Primary is a huge school."

"I've been on a course this afternoon with a teacher who works there, and she says they are likely to replace it with a much smaller school. If that happens, they think that an extension will be built at St Marks to accommodate the children who they can't take in their smaller replacement building."

This story seemed incredible, so the next morning I telephoned the head mistress of Beech Street to check up on it. She confirmed the rumours. Major structural faults had indeed been discovered in her building, although at present it could still be used. The cost of repairs was likely to be high so it seemed sensible to build a modern replacement school within the existing grounds. Pupils and staff would move into it when it was completed, and the old building would then be demolished. There was no suggestion that St Marks would be affected in any way.

That evening, I repeated the Head's account to Anita, and remarked that the rest was obviously idle speculation. I soon had to eat my own words! Two days later I attended a meeting after school, and sat next to a head teacher whose own school was being extended. During a coffee break, I asked him how the work was progressing.

"Oh . . . very slowly," he replied wearily, and we talked for a while about the difficulties he was experiencing.

"Buildings are in the news recently," I quipped. "What with yours being enlarged and Beech Street Primary on the point of collapse!"

"And you are to have a new extension built," he added, in a very matter-of-fact way.

"Who told you that?" I asked in astonishment.

He mentioned the name of an education officer in the School Buildings Department, saying, "Mr Carlson told me about it last week, as we were looking round my school together."

The following morning, the local newspaper bore a headline:

CALL TO DEMOLISH
BEECH STREET SCHOOL

It went on to describe how serious structural faults had been found in the building and that there were plans to knock it down. The replacement school would be smaller, and two extra teachers would be employed at St Marks to cope with "surplus children" from Beech Street.

When I arrived at school, I found a note on my pad to the effect that Mr Thomas, a senior education officer, had telephoned, and I knew immediately what the call had been about.

I contacted him and a lengthy discussion followed. He embarked on a long, complicated explanation stressing that there were still "many hurdles" to get over before any work could begin on the project at Beech Street.

"The local newspaper has jumped in *far* too quickly," he concluded. "It has given the impression we are ready to go ahead."

When he had finished, I left him in no doubt about my feelings on the subject. I did not appreciate reading about plans for my own school in the local paper, or hearing the news from other heads, when neither the School Governors nor I had been given any information by the Education Office. I underlined the point (yet again) that the physical provision at St Marks had always been sub-standard, and that if an extension *were* to be built, some thought should be given to upgrading the rest of the building at the same time!

CHAPTER
NINE

A Shaky Start

One Monday morning in early October, I walked into my office and saw a hurriedly-scribbled note lying on my desk. It read:

"Sunday night 11.50p.m.
Called out to fire in dustbin area.
One fire engine came — now waiting for police.
Fireman states there is no serious damage to woodwork.
Asked if I would wait for police to come to make an official report."

I immediately recognised the handwriting as that of Joe Jackson, the caretaker, and I had barely finished reading his note when he appeared at my door looking tired and disgruntled.

He told me that shortly after 11.30 on the previous night, he had received a telephone call at home telling him the school dustbins were ablaze, and that the fire brigade had been summoned. He had hurried to school, a distance of about a quarter of a mile, to find that the story was true, but that the fire engine had not yet arrived.

He had begun to unwind and connect up the hosepipe that he used around the school, and had almost completed the task when a fire engine had come racing to the scene. The fire was soon put out, but even though he waited at school until 12.30a.m., no police officers had appeared.

It was obvious that the fire had been started deliberately, and that the culprits were not small children. Joe's opinion was that two or three young men, returning home after a night out, had fired the dustbins for "a lark". We had had a similar incident the previous year when the wooden partition separating the dustbin area from the waste food area outside the kitchen had been burnt to ashes.

By coincidence, that very afternoon I was visited by a member of the fire service to see if I was willing to promote the "Welephant Club". This was a fire service initiative designed to alert young children to the dangers of fire, to help them recognise potential hazards in the home, and to emphasise the foolishness and danger of making false alarm calls.

"A fire prevention officer will come to the school accompanied by another officer dressed in a seven-foot elephant costume," explained my visitor. "The officer and the 'Welephant' character do a sort of double act and we invite the children to join our Club, giving out free badges, stickers and colouring sheets."

"But why an elephant?" I asked, rather perplexed.

"Because it has a trunk and squirts water, sir!"

Of course I welcomed the visit, but later, reflecting on the day's events, I found it paradoxical that at the same time as energy was being put into this initiative for children, supposedly mature adults were involved in putting buildings at risk by their irresponsible behaviour.

As to the non-arrival of any police support following the incident, Joe expressed his opinion of the force in no uncertain terms.

"Well, they wouldn't have caught them anyway," he said grumpily.

Our second crisis hit us less than two weeks later! It was a very wet Thursday morning, and everyone had arrived at school buttoned into waterproof coats or clutching umbrellas.

Half an hour after morning lessons had begun, Joe suddenly appeared at my office door bearing a mop, a bucket and a very worried look.

"Water is pouring into Homebase 2!" he exclaimed tersely and disappeared in the direction of that classroom.

Thirty seconds later, having rushed out after him, I was standing at the edge of Class 2 work bay watching an expanding pool of water creep across the blue carpeted floor. As Joe dashed away to get some material to soak up the water, Vincent Leach appeared with another mop and bucket and began to stem the flow which by this time had reached the edge of the carpet and was pushing long wet fingers across the adjacent lino-tiles. Suddenly, a great shower of water cascaded down from a corner of the ceiling, close to an internal drainpipe, narrowly missing a bookcase full of reading books.

Moments later, Joe reappeared in his green waterproofs and wellington boots on his way to the roof, and soon after he had disappeared up the ladder, the flow of water decreased considerably. At about the same time, the sky brightened, the heavy rain ceased and the miniature waterfall was reduced to a trickle.

Other members of staff, attracted by the frenzied activity, had left their own classes to discover its cause. Together they began to move Homebase 2's furniture, books and equipment to a drier part of the building. Moments later, Joe reappeared and reported that some lead flashing was missing from around the top of one of the drainpipes, but he had managed to make a temporary repair.

Predictably, the next couple of days were difficult for everyone. The displaced class was relocated to a temporary base but the pupils were unsettled by the change, and other children in the school were distracted by the necessary alterations in routine. Joe worked unstintingly to absorb as much water as possible from the carpet (which was glued to the floor!) and offered to put in extra hours during the weekend to move the furniture back and make Homebase 2 habitable once more.

However, when I contacted the "Office" to explain what had happened and to arrange for Joe's overtime payments, I met with begrudging attitudes and a reluctance to pay him for his efforts. Nevertheless, I dug my heels in and insisted that two hours overtime be approved, so that Homebase 2 would ready for use by Monday morning.

So, the Autumn term was barely a month old, and we had already coped with two crises! I knew that I needed to be as upbeat as possible to counteract their discouraging effect. One positive step would be to reinstate the "Craft Afternoons" which had been so successful in previous years.

During these sessions, pupils from our "top class" worked on various crafts in different parts of the open-plan building. They developed a wide range of skills and techniques using different materials. In previous years, our older children had looked forward to these weekly lessons and had achieved first class results, respecting and obeying the adult helpers who had come in to work with them.

This year, I had delayed the start of the project as I was not sure that we would have enough adults to staff it. In previous years, Reverend Strong had taken a group of children, but he would not be able to do so this time as he was on a course. In addition, two mothers who had given help in the past had found jobs during the holiday so they too would be unavailable.

Nevertheless, a little serious recruiting by Vincent and myself resulted in four new volunteers joining us, and having got six leaders we were able to go ahead with our plans.

The children were divided into groups of 5 or 6 and were offered a number of activities on which they would work for half a term, before changing to a new activity.

They could choose from:

- Woodwork — making model aeroplanes, pencil boxes, dolls' furniture, etc., using balsa wood and simple tools, such as metal rulers, small saws, knives and glass paper.
- Pottery — modelling, painting and glazing coil pots, thumb pots and small figurines using real clay and firing them in our small kiln, which was installed in the new building in 1974 but not used for several years.
- Mosaic work — decorating teapot stands, plant holders and table lamps by covering them with small pieces of broken tile or pottery and rubbing grout into the cracks.
- Tie and dye work — beginning with decorating handkerchiefs and progressing to scarves, blouses and even shirts.
- Cookery — usually baking cakes or biscuits, using a small Baby Belling cooker which could be plugged into an ordinary wall socket.
- Embroidery — drawing simple patterns on napkins or place-mats and using different coloured silks to decorate them.
- Sewing — which usually consisted of soft toy making, working from patterns.
- Knitting — with the emphasis once again on making dolls and other toys.

Sometimes, in the past, we had provided all these activities simultaneously; at other times, a selection from them, depending on the number, interests and abilities of the helpers.

The day of the first session came. The children, who had been eagerly looking forward to the experience for several days, worked hard and behaved perfectly, and the new helpers — two mothers and two school meal supervisors — quickly found their feet and, at the end of the session, told me they had thoroughly enjoyed themselves.

"At last," I thought. "Things are looking up!" And I began to look forward to the Harvest Festival Service, which was due to take place in five days time.

As soon as Joe Jackson arrived at school on the following Tuesday morning, he put out all the chairs in the school hall. By 9.30a.m., half of them were already occupied by parents and grandparents who had arrived early and were waiting for the Harvest Service to begin at 10 o'clock. In 1974, when the school first opened, one rarely saw a man at a day-time event, but ten years on, a lot of fathers had been able to come, possibly because of the high level of unemployment in the area.

There was a buzz of excitement from all the Homebases as registers were called, and suppressed exclamations of "Shhhhhhh!" from the teachers as, at 9.55a.m., the children formed lines and moved in an orderly fashion towards the hall.

When all the children were in place, I welcomed everyone and announced that the theme of this year's service would be "Water" — very topical in view of the long hot summer, the empty reservoirs and the threat of standpipes in some parts of the country. The performance clicked into action and went through without a hitch. The children behaved well throughout the service and tried hard in all their activities.

Each junior class performed a song, a poem or a sketch presenting either ways in which water had been used throughout the ages or the poverty and hardship suffered by people in other countries where water was scarce.

Eventually, however, it was the turn of the Reception class. These infant children usually cause a great deal of amusement amongst the audience, and they certainly lived up to expectations this time! Their lack of inhibition, and unpredictable actions — such as waving to parents unexpectedly or singing over-enthusiastically — created many comical situations. They sang several short action songs and were a rousing success.

Reverend Strong's contribution was a short story entitled: A Drink of Water. As he finished, much to his surprise, he received an enthusiastic round of applause from the parents, and the Harvest Service ended with all the children singing one of their favourite songs: The Water of Life.

That evening I returned to school for the termly meeting of the School Governors at 7.30p.m. The agenda covered mainly routine matters, but one item interested me greatly. It was a proposal by the Education Office to build an extension to our school.

Following the initial article in our local paper, Reverend Strong and I had sent an official report to the Chief Education Officer, clearly stating the need for upgraded facilities at St Marks. I circulated copies of the letter we had sent around the group.

I passed round, too, a sketch plan showing how further amenities could be added to our present building. The governors studied the drawing for some time whilst I explained various points and answered questions. It was unanimously agreed that copies of my drawing should be sent to the Buildings Department at the Education Office, so that senior officers might get some idea of the extent of our plans.

When the November half-term holiday arrived, everyone on the staff, including myself, felt in need of a break. We had weathered various crises and several teachers had been affected by a virulent strain of the common cold that had travelled around the staff.

I hoped that after a week's rest and recuperation everyone would return fighting fit and ready to engage in the hectic, though enjoyable, lead-up to Christmas.

CHAPTER
TEN

Difficult Days

"To strike or not to strike, that is the question," misquoted Anita, as we listened to the radio news over breakfast during the half-term break.

For weeks there had been rumblings from the teachers' unions — the NUT in particular — about taking industrial action if their latest demands were not met. Most teachers had been bitterly disappointed by the 1984 arbitration settlement of 5.1%, and discussions on a 1985 deal were now running into problems. The employers intended to link any future salary increase to changes in teachers' conditions of service — and in particular, to the introduction of teacher appraisal.

"I don't think I'll go on strike even if everyone else does," said Anita. "It's wrong to close schools. Some children, whose parents are at work, could end up roaming the streets."

I nodded. "I hope it doesn't come to that," I said, "but it sounds as though there's trouble ahead!"

In fact trouble seemed to be already with us! For in addition to the threatened strike, every week the local newspaper seemed to publish rumours and speculation about Beech Street School and the various ways in which St Marks might be affected. Beech Street structural faults were to cost £270,000, St Marks' extension was to cost £57,000 and, only to add to the confusion, Beech Street School was a grade 2 listed building designed by a well-known local architect.

"To demolish it would be an act of vandalism," protested some local councilors and dignitaries.

"What will you do if there *is* a strike?" asked Anita.

I shrugged my shoulders.

"There's not a lot I can do! From my point of view it would be best if *all* the teachers were to go on strike, then the school would have to close. My worst scenario would be a staff split — I don't know how we would cope if some teachers came into work and others took industrial action."

"I doubt it will come to that," said Anita confidently.

On the first day back after the half-term break, I drove into the car park at the same time as Vincent Leach. As we walked in together, he told me that he had been having increasing trouble with his right eye and that the only available appointment with his optician was in the middle of the day. He had booked a session during lunchtime and would be out of school for 45 minutes. I knew that he had been having recurrent eye discomfort for several weeks, so I understood his anxiety to have it checked out as soon as possible.

Vincent left for his appointment at lunchtime, intending to return before afternoon school. At 1.15p.m., I took a call from him. His optician had discovered a haemorrage behind his right eye, and he had to see his G.P. immediately. The condition was serious and needed to be treated with some urgency.

I expressed my concern and, as soon as Vincent rang off, checked my diary. There were no visitors due that afternoon, so I quickly prepared some work to occupy Vincent's class. By the time the afternoon bell sounded, I was sitting at his desk ready to complete the afternoon register. To my surprise, just half an hour later, Vincent arrived. His G. P. was out on visits and would not be available until 4p.m. — so he had decided to come into school!

That evening, Vincent rang me at home to say that he would be in school as usual on the following day. He had been given an out-patient's appointment at the local hospital in a week's time — so much for "urgent treatment"! However, I realised that his eye condition might result in prolonged absences in the near future.

Towards the end of November, a sad and distressing affair came to light concerning a girl in the top class. It began one Tuesday morning when the girl's stepmother was found wandering around the Homebases by Cathy Green and her nursery assistant Diane Davies.

They asked her if they could help in any way, and she replied that she was looking for her stepdaughter, Sophie Ellwood. She said she had an appointment to take her "somewhere" during the afternoon. The parent seemed furtive and evasive. The teachers were disturbed by her unusual and secretive behaviour and reported the matter to me. The following day, Sophie came to my office to ask permission to leave school during the afternoon.

"I have to go somewhere with my mum, but I haven't to tell anyone about it at all," she explained dramatically.

Having established that she would be picked up from her Homebase by her stepmother at a pre-arranged time, I agreed she could leave and made no further enquiries.

The following morning, a social worker rang to tell me that the girl's father had been arrested the previous afternoon and charged with seriously assaulting her on several occasions two years previously, when she and her sister were living alone with him following his divorce from their mother.

Months later, the father had remarried and Sophie, her sister, their father and their new stepmother had settled down in a new home together. Recently, a new baby had been born, following which Sophie had told her stepmother about the assaults and, appalled at what she had heard, she had contacted the police.

The father had been given bail on condition that he lived away from his home and made no attempts to see his children. The case had been referred to the Crown Court and would be heard in due course.

At lunchtime, during a short staff meeting, I gave the teachers the facts, stressing their confidential nature and informing them of the court's ruling. Without going into detail, I instructed the three meals supervisors that on no account must either of the girls be spoken to or collected by their father during lunch periods. This was not too surprising for them as it can sometimes be the procedure in the event of marital breakdown.

A few days later, I was invited by the N.S.P.C.C. to attend a conference to discuss the case of Sophie Ellwood. There were practical questions needing to be resolved, such as who would have legal custody of Sophie and her sister, and matters concerning their financial support. Having been made aware of the traumatic episodes that had been part of Sophie's home life, I was haunted by the frightening and oppressive circumstances that such a young girl had had to endure.

However, we all had to put our darker feelings to one side as December was fast approaching, and we had to firm up our Christmas plans. No matter how many problems arose, we could not disappoint our children or their parents.

One of our first tasks was to buy the Christmas tree. Joe and I planned to visit our local garden centre to choose a suitable specimen. However, on the morning in question, I arrived at school to find a great deal of broken glass scattered along the drive and over the car park. Empty milk bottles, left out overnight for early collection by the milkman, had been smashed on the concrete forecourt.

Inside the building, Joe greeted me with the news that 5 large windows in Homebase 5 had also been smashed and although he had picked up the fragments of glass from the area, the missing panes were allowing the classroom to feel cold and inhospitable.

Naturally, our tree-buying plans were put on hold until the windows were boarded up, but during the afternoon we were able to get away for an hour and returned with a fine six-foot specimen. We wedged it into a large plastic tub so that Reception Class could decorate it on the following morning under the supervision of Cathy and Diane.

Several events had been arranged leading up to Christmas. In the first week of December there was to be a "Mince Pie Morning" when parents would be invited into school to listen to our younger children singing seasonal songs and carols, and enjoy a mince pie and a cup of coffee.

Then, much nearer to Christmas we would hold a Christmas Concert in which every class would play its part. There was such a demand for seats that we had to issue tickets — 2 per family. However, we usually had a dress rehearsal during the afternoon of the previous day, to which we invited grandparents and residents of the local old people's home — so nobody really "missed out".

Last, but not least, there were two Christmas parties for the children — with a special white-bearded, red-coated visitor hopefully appearing at the one arranged for our two infant classes.

In early December, Vincent visited the outpatient's clinic for his scheduled appointment and rang me at home to say that he was staying in hospital to undergo tests, including a brain scan. There had been no improvement in his eye condition, and he thought it unlikely that he would be in school again before Christmas. To add to his personal burden he had learned that day that his mother had terminal cancer, and had a life expectancy of only two months.

This was all grim news for Vincent. I understood his position and empathised with his serious problems, but at a personal level his continuing absence made life increasingly difficult for me. I had a senior class without a teacher just as we were embarking on one of the busiest times of the school year.

Fortunately, I knew of a good supply teacher who, I hoped, was not employed at the time. As soon as Vincent had finished speaking, I rang up Brenda Pilling.

Brenda had worked at St Marks for several years before leaving a year or so earlier. She was nowhere near retirement age, but she and her husband had decided that, as they had no children, it was financially unnecessary for both of them to work, and Brenda was very happy to be the homemaker. However, she was always willing to help us out in a crisis, and had popped in and out regularly over the previous twelve months. I told her about Vincent's extended absence, which might well last until after Christmas, and asked if she felt able to take on his class. When she agreed to do so, it was as if a burden had been lifted from my shoulders. Not only was Brenda familiar with our ways of working, but most of our older pupils remembered and respected her. She took over from me two days later (the authority rule being that schools had to "manage" for two days without a replacement teacher), and with great relief I began to focus on getting through Christmas with no more disturbances or disasters.

My spirits were further lifted a day or two later when the mother of two of our pupils came to see me.

"My husband has a disco player at home complete with coloured, flashing lights," she said. "He usually does weddings, birthdays and anniversaries. He would be happy to set it up for the children's school parties if you'd like him to. He'd do it for nothing of course — free of charge."

I thought quickly. Whilst a disco might not be suitable for the Infant Party — when games such as The Farmer in his Den, Pass the Parcel and Musical Chairs were the highlight of the afternoon — the older children were very much into *Top of the Pops*, and I was sure they would appreciate a disco session before they went home.

I thanked her for the offer and arranged for her husband to arrive during the "party tea" to set up his equipment ready for the more energetic second half of the afternoon.

As the days flew by, school took on a festive appearance, with coloured streamers hung across Homebases and seasonal scenes painted onto the long windows. The children were becoming more and more excited. Every day there was a short Concert rehearsal, and during the lunch period, teachers — with the help of some parents — fitted home-made costumes on to children who were taking starring parts in the show.

Dress rehearsal day arrived, and by 2p.m. the school hall was filled by grandparents and residents from the sheltered accommodation just a hundred yards from the school. It was difficult to keep the children calm as their excitement was reaching fever pitch. But, once the show began, everything went according to plan. The grey-haired audience thoroughly enjoyed their afternoon out, and we crossed our fingers in the hope that everything would run just as smoothly on the night of the "big performance".

The following evening, even though the concert was not due to begin until 7p.m., parents began to arrive before 6.30p.m. Although tickets had been issued to guarantee admission, the seats were not numbered and could not be reserved — so it was a case of first come, first served. And some parents were determined to get the *best* seats on the *front* row!

The programme, which lasted for just over an hour, consisted of a number of playlets linked musically by songs or carols. From experience we had learned that separate items were better than one continuous show. Each section could be rehearsed independently by the class involved, and every child in the school would be able to take part in some way.

The first sketch, entitled *Mrs Beeton's Christmas Kitchen*, was performed by the older children, and our younger juniors presented *When Santa Got Stuck Up the Chimney*, which could best be described as a seasonal farce! The older infants acted out the story of The Snowman's Special Christmas in which a lonely snowman is visited by his fairy godmother and becomes

101

so happy that "he melts with a smile on his face". Finally the Reception Class performed the Nativity, which brought a tear to everyone's eye and loud crying from one of the shepherds who was overcome by the occasion!

Everything went well, and at the end of the evening, Janet Clarke — our pianist and severest critic — gave her unqualified approval.

"That was excellent!" she said and went home smiling.

On the day following the Christmas Concert, Mrs Mullen, the school clerk, was absent from school with a heavy cold. Therefore my first job of the morning was to collect "bank money" from the children and go out to the bank to pay it in. As this was the last bank day before the Christmas holiday, deposits were a mere £3.55 whilst withdrawals amounted to £58!

After my visit to the bank, I toured Merringham in order to buy certain essentials for the children's Christmas parties, returning with 12 litres of ice cream (which were stored in the kitchen freezer), several packets of serviettes and 3 lbs of sweets to serve as prizes. This was before the days of being "tooth-friendly"!

The following afternoon, we held the party for our infants. They had great fun playing pass the parcel, musical mats and circle games such as "There was a Princess long ago", and chattered excitedly as they ate the party tea of sandwiches, cake, jelly and ice cream.

Despite all our efforts, we had been unable to find a suitable, and available, candidate to play Father Christmas at the party. The teachers had reluctantly decided to give each child a small bag of sweets and simply wish them "A Merry Christmas". Then, quite unexpectedly, during the morning of the party, "Santa Claus" was discovered to be living very close to school! A parent who was a regular helper came in to tell us that one of her neighbours had played the part in a local nursery a few days previously and, with a little gentle persuasion from her, had agreed to visit St Marks at 3.30p.m. — requiring me to make another (express) tour of Merringham to find several dozen little gifts, which the teachers wrapped during their lunch hour.

The Junior party was held on the following afternoon, and began with a fancy dress parade! The children had been anticipating the event for days. During the lunch hour, they retired to their Homebases to put on costumes made of paper, cardboard or ordinary household items. The teachers had decided that a prize should be given for the most original costumes — and so that they might be seen to be impartial, it was my responsibility to judge them!

Most costumes although amusing, could be quickly eliminated, but I found it almost impossible to decide between the four finalists. One girl entered as a fisherwoman, equipped with wellington boots, a rod, a net and a waterproof coat. Another made a very creditable "Aunt Sally" from the Worzel Gummidge T.V. series. A third was a garden gnome, complete with pointed hat, green tunic and hose. The fourth was a boy, complete with curlers, apron and headscarf, masquerading as a character from T.V.'s Coronation Street. Eventually, I awarded first prize to the boy, and the three girls received prizes as joint runners-up.

After tea, our volunteer "disc jockey" entertained the children for over an hour with his disco-player. I had looked forward to seeing his performance, but I stayed in the hall for only a few minutes once the disco had begun. The combined effects of flashing coloured lights, repetitive drumming music and incomprehensible chatter over the microphone brought on an instant headache! Nevertheless, the children danced enthusiastically, greatly enjoying the cacophony, and gave three rousing cheers as the last record ended the party.

The following day was the last day of term. The day when crepe decorations and coloured paper chains are taken down to fill waste paper bins around the school. The day when snowmen, Santas and holly, lovingly painted on classroom windows but a short time ago are washed into oblivion with soapy water. The day when the Christmas tree is stripped, and coloured lights, baubles and tinsel are packed into boxes to spend another year in the school loft.

It was also the day of the school Christmas dinner. When the lunchtime bell rang, the children formed a long queue which wavered from side to side with excitement. But having anticipated the feast, many children did not appreciate the traditional Christmas fare, and great quantities of Brussels sprouts and

Christmas pudding were returned to the kitchen untouched.

The staff had supervised the children whilst they ate (or didn't eat) their meal. When they went out to play we adults sat down together to enjoy ours in a more peaceful atmosphere. Reverend Strong had joined us, and we began our lunch at around 12.40p.m. I had provided wine, and Janet had contributed some after-dinner mints, and the menu of pork, stuffing, apple sauce, sprouts, roast and mashed potatoes followed by plum pudding and white sauce was enjoyed by all. The conversation around the table was light-hearted and convivial, despite the fact that many of the teachers looked tired and drawn after a long and difficult term.

At 3.00p.m., the children gathered in the school hall for a final assembly. They sang *The Twelve Days of Christmas* (speeding up as they progressed through the verses) and Reverend Strong said a final prayer. The day ended on a happy note as all the children went home to go through the fun of decorations and feasting all over again with their own families.

At 4.15p.m., I said goodbye to Brenda Pilling, our faithful supply teacher, thanking her and telling her that I was anticipating Vincent's return in the New Year. However, as she left we exchanged a few wry comments, knowing that she would probably be coming in to cover for another absence before very long.

CHAPTER
ELEVEN

Fire and Snow

Anita and I awoke on the first day of the Christmas holiday to reports on the national news of a major fire in the Summit Railway Tunnel between Littleborough and Todmorden — the longest tunnel in England. A freight train carrying 13 tankers of petrol had entered the tunnel on the Yorkshire side and been derailed. One of the tankers had fallen on its side and begun to leak petrol into the tunnel and this had been ignited by a hot axle box on the engine.

The tunnel was only a few miles from where we lived so everyone locally was agog at the news. There were reports of huge pillars of flame rising 100 feet into the air from the huge cylindrical brick ventilation shafts on the hillside above the line. I was particularly interested to hear all the details because, having been born in Littleborough, I knew the area well and as a child had often walked over the hills and seen the ventilation shafts. There were several of them, at 200 yard intervals, marching in a line across the moorland heather. Fortunately, no one was killed in the incident, but the railway line was closed for many months following the episode.

★ ★ ★

The fire was a temporary distraction from the situation at St Marks. For weeks I had been worrying about problems that were constantly arising at school. Rumours about the rebuilding of Beech Street and our possible extension were rumbling on — although I had heard nothing official — and the combined threats of vandalism, a teachers' strike and Vincent's prolonged absences were getting me down.

Anita — always sensitive to my moods — had picked up the signs.

"Let's have a really restful holiday," she said on the third day of our break, as we were decorating our little Christmas tree. "The only major event we are responsible for is the family Boxing Day buffet party; the rest of the time we can enjoy other people's hospitality and take long walks around Hollingworth Lake or over the moors."

That seemed a very positive suggestion, so I tried to relax and follow her advice. Christmas Eve came and went without incident and on Christmas Day, after going to church in the morning, we ate Christmas dinner with our immediate family. Crackers were pulled, presents were opened, relatives were telephoned and thanked, and the day passed off happily.

On Boxing Day, Anita and I were up with the larks, preparing the various dishes for our buffet. It had become a tradition for us to invite relatives and friends to spend the afternoon and evening with us — Anita's mother, our sisters Maureen and Pam and their husbands, friends from church, one or two elderly

107

couples who had to be collected by car, and my mother who, having been widowed two years previously, now lived alone. As you might imagine, the party was a relatively sedate affair, but nonetheless enjoyable. There was relaxed conversation; talk of Christmases long past; one or two pencil and paper games; repeated visits to the buffet table, and the sipping of several glasses of wine. By 10.30p.m., most of our visitors were putting on their coats and saying their goodbyes.

A friend from church, who lived not far from my mother's house in Littleborough, had offered to drive her home so that I too could relax and enjoy a glass of wine. At 11.00p.m., we waved them both off as Sheila reversed her car out of our drive. Later, as Anita and I started on the mountain of dirty dishes, we agreed that it had been a tiring but very enjoyable day.

The next morning, I had a brief telephone conversation with my Mum, then Anita and I visited a fruit tree nursery in search of new plants for our garden. At last, I was beginning to unwind and was cheered by the fact that I wasn't due to return to school until the end of the first week in January. I still had two weeks before I needed to think about work!

During the afternoon, my sister rang to say she couldn't get hold of Mum, but I reassured her, saying that I had spoken to her that morning and she was well — I suggested that she had probably gone to visit her cousin. However, when she was still not answering the phone in the early evening, I decided to drive over to Littleborough with Anita just to make sure everything was alright.

What a shock we had when we went in. After our morning conversation, Mum must have felt unwell. She had got back into bed and died. She had made no attempt to use her bed-side phone, and the bedcovers lay smoothly. She was at peace. Although we did not think it at the time, on reflection we were comforted by the fact that she had spent her last day surrounded by family and friends and had thoroughly enjoyed our Boxing Day buffet — especially the Black Forest gateau, her favourite!

I telephoned my sister, and she and her husband drove over to join us. The arrival of the police, the ambulance and the undertaker meant that there was no sleep for any of us that night. In the days that followed, the collection of certificates and the funeral arrangements seemed to take up every waking moment and, as Mum's house was now empty, we felt we had to remove various papers and items as soon as possible.

In short, the relaxing break away from school had not materialised — in fact it had become a deeply distressing time for all of us.

When school re-opened on the 7th January, the staff, including Vincent, arrived bright and early in spite of the dreadful weather. Everywhere was covered with a thick layer of snow, and the children came to school clothed in heavy outdoor coats, scarves and wellington boots. During playtime, I learnt that Vincent was still taking medication for his eye condition, which had not yet fully recovered, and that his mother's health was gradually deteriorating.

During the Christmas break, I had realised that the school computer had remained virtually untouched since its delivery the previous August. Although some teachers had tried to familiarise themselves with it, they had been just too busy planning lessons, marking books and arranging events to integrate its use into their lessons. In order to help the situation, I decided to withdraw a group of 4 or 5 children from the top class each day and spend an hour showing them how the computer worked. Most children had never seen a computer before, so my "lessons" included how to switch it on, how to use the keyboard, and how to load a programme from a disc. Basic though they were, the children enjoyed these sessions immensely and soon learned the skills and techniques needed to use the machine. The computer trolley was parked just outside my office door, so I was still able to answer the telephone or welcome visitors as necessary.

We had been at school for less than a week when Vincent rang me at home to tell me that his mother had died in hospital and that he would be absent from school for a day or two. Once again I rang Brenda Pilling to arrange cover for his absence, but had only just replaced the receiver when Janet Clarke telephoned to say that she too would be absent with a heavy cold.

I drove to school the following morning wondering what on earth would happen next. In the event we coped reasonably well, but I was aware that such a lack of continuity must be affecting the children's education, as supply teachers often resorted to time-consuming tasks or implemented inappropriate activities as they "stood in" for a day. But there seemed to be very little that could be done about it.

During most of January, snow lay on the ground, occasionally topped up by additional flurries which fell unexpectedly and caught everyone out.

Capitalising on the situation, ever-creative Cathy introduced a new theme to her class entitled "Snow", and her five-year-olds arrived at school each morning excited at the prospect of some new activity.

One morning, two little girls came to my office and invited me to watch their "Snow Dance" — movement and mime to taped music — which the class was to perform in the school hall during the afternoon. It was based on the story by Raymond Briggs in which a little boy builds a snowman that comes to life and befriends him. The boy and the snowman take a flight over the town and continue to the North Pole where they meet Father Christmas. On their return, the snowman melts, leaving the boy with only memories and a blue scarf given to him by Santa.

I accepted the invitation and promised to be there in the school hall after lunch to see their performance. Just as I was about to go to the hall, a boy from the top class arrived at my office door with blood streaming from a head wound. He had been sliding down an embankment on a layer of crisp snow, had collided with another boy, and been deflected into a tree. Although the cut was less than an inch long, it appeared to be very deep, so I telephoned his mother, picked her up

111

and drove them both to the casualty department of the local hospital.

I left them in the waiting room and hurried back to school to see the last 10 minutes of the "Snow Dance" — much to the children's delight — and half an hour later was joined by the "wounded soldier" who had returned from hospital wearing a hero's grin and a row of butterfly plasters across his forehead.

Over the next two weeks, Cathy developed the "Snow" theme. She converted a corner of her Homebase into "The Snowman's House". With the help of Joe Jackson, she put up a white polythene screen and incorporated into it a snowman-shaped doorway, furnishing the room with white tables and chairs. Children could use this area to read and to write but they had to agree to be completely quiet, as Cathy told them the snowman did not like noise.

Their imaginations were fired by this innovation, and they produced some very good pieces of work. But when messages from "Mr Snowman" appeared in the "house" on some mornings, the children became very excited indeed.

Cathy thought hard how she could bring her theme to a satisfactory end to make way for another topic. She eventually decided that a personal appearance by the snowman would be both a fitting and an exciting conclusion. With this in mind, she had a long conversation with Joe.

One Friday lunchtime, a few days later, I walked into the staffroom to find Cathy and nursery assistant Diane helping Joe into a voluminous white costume — which enveloped him completely — in preparation for the appearance of "Mr Snowman" in Homebase 1.

When the bell announced the start of afternoon lessons, Cathy shepherded the children together outside her work bay and told them that a special guest had arrived. In response to the children's excited questions, Cathy confirmed that the visitor was indeed "Mr Snowman" who was in his "house" and had come to say goodbye to the class before melting to make way for spring. She impressed upon the children that "Mr Snowman" could not speak to them but would shake each one of them by the hand. This is, in fact, what happened, and ten minutes later "Mr Snowman" had departed, leaving behind 33 very excited children, and a damp patch on the carpet — a touch of realism dreamt up by Joe, who had insisted on secreting some wet sponges inside his costume!

This January topic had been educationally invaluable. In the children it had inspired creativity, and practised discipline and respect. It had been a magical experience for them all.

By contrast, the end of January realised my worst fears when Janet, the National Union of Teachers' representative at St Marks, told me that she had received notice that her members were being asked to take industrial action in a week's time in support of their pay claim. They were advised to refuse to take classes for absent colleagues, refuse to attend all staff meetings and out-of-school activities, and to withdraw from the supervision of school meals.

There were four NUT members on the staff and, although not particularly militant or disruptive, they felt they had no alternative other than to follow the Union's recommendations. Other staff members — not in the NUT — refused to take on extra duties as that would diminish the effects of the industrial action.

The next day, I drafted out a letter to parents explaining that groups of children were likely to be excluded from school during coming weeks, and that our Parents' Evening, planned to take place in mid February, would have to be postponed. I telephoned the Chairman of Governors, Reverend Strong, to tell him of the impending action and explain that after all, the school would not be able to take part in the Church's Centenary Celebrations.

Apart from the obvious disruption which was bound to take place, the action also meant that I would have to supervise the school meal every day. Although we had 3 "dinner ladies", they did not carry enough authority to deal with any disciplinary problems that might occur. Under normal circumstances, teachers having a school meal would supervise the children as they ate, but as they were now withdrawing from school meals (and were advised to leave the building), they would not be in the hall at lunch time, so even the influence of their presence would be missing.

The spring meeting of the school governors took place about a week after the "work to rule" had begun. It was a very quiet one. Everyone knew the teachers' action was bound to restrict the school's activities, but little was said about it because everyone also knew there was nothing I personally could do about it.

There had been no further communication from the Education Office about our school extension — another disappointment — and the only matter which took up more than five minutes was a proposal by the Secretary of State for Education and Science to change the composition of school governing bodies so that more "interested parties" were included. In St Mark's case this would double the size of the governing body from 6 to 12 and require the election of 2 parent governors and 1 teacher governor. It was approved unanimously.

CHAPTER
TWELVE

Life Savers

At that time, Government decreed that all primary schools should hold "a daily act of corporate worship." Although the morning assembly at St Marks was occasionally led by a group of children, and from time to time by Reverend Strong, under normal circumstances the "corporate worship" was down to me.

Because of the wide age range within the school, there were in fact two assemblies on most days of the week. Janet and Cathy took an infant assembly in one of their Homebases on Mondays, Tuesdays, Thursdays and Fridays, whilst I led morning assembly for the junior classes in the school hall.

On Wednesdays, however, we all came together for a joint assembly when children could show what they had achieved during the week. Sometimes a group would bring in pictures they had painted, or individual children would read out poems or stories they had written. Occasionally, children would sing a song, tell about a class project or give a report on an educational visit.

It was also the morning when "Merit Mark" winners were announced. These marks rewarded excellent progress, good behaviour or outstanding effort by children of all educational abilities. Teachers awarded Merit Marks during the week, and the recipients were asked to stand in assembly on Wednesday mornings and receive the praise they deserved. This system of Merit Marks monitored a child's cooperation, effort and progress within school. The total number of Merit Marks gained in the year was noted in the Report Books which were sent out to parents just before the summer holiday.

When planning Junior assemblies, I tried hard to think of topics that would interest them. As a class teacher, I had sat through too many assemblies which were ritualistic, boring, or merely an opportunity to harangue children for bad behaviour.

Coming up with something new and fresh on 4 days every week was not an easy task, and I gathered together mountains of material from a variety of sources. There were Saints Days which often provided a story to be told. There were the familiar stories of Christmas, Easter and Pentecost at the appropriate times of the year. Old Testament tales often contained lessons in right behaviour, and there were tales of bravery or persistence with more modern role models such as William Wilberforce, Grace Darling, Mother Teresa, or Martin Luther King.

The changing seasons were another source of inspiration. In spring there were new babies, new life and the wonders of creation; in autumn the harvest, hibernation and our good fortune at having warmth and shelter, in contrast with some people in other parts of the world who were experiencing hardship or famine.

One morning, as part of a theme on "Bravery", I told the story of José, a young Spanish boy who arrived home one day to find his house on fire. Such was his presence of mind and speed of thought that he dashed through the flames into the kitchen and carried out a large cylinder of gas which, had it exploded, would have put neighbouring buildings at risk.

Even before the assembly, I had personal doubts as to whether the boy's action should be regarded as courageous or foolhardy, so having related the story, I asked for the children's opinion. They unanimously agreed that the story portrayed an act of great bravery!

As I brought the assembly to a close, I remarked that José's action may well have saved many people's lives, and asked if there were any children present who had saved a person's life. I had expected a negative response, and was astonished to find that several children raised their hands immediately in reply to my question.

The following morning, the assembly centred around 3 pupils who had replied positively to my question, and whose prompt action had averted disaster. I had asked them all to make notes so that they would not be overcome by nerves, and they told their stories as follows:

James (aged 8 years):
It was the day of my birthday. We were all playing outside in the sun, because it was summer then. We

118

were waiting for my party to start really, but my Mum hadn't called us in, because she wasn't quite ready. Well, I saw this big green car come zooming round the corner, and my little sister who is three was just stepping into the road. I ran at my sister and just grabbed her, and rushed across the road. We sort of rolled over on the grass at the other side of the road, and the car went flying past. He was a madcap driver.

Tessa (aged 9 years):

I was with my friend in our street. I had asked Nathan's Mum if I could play with him. He's only three. We were all playing, and suddenly Nathan disappeared. I went into the house to look for Nathan, and he was just going up to the cooker to get hold of a pan. I ran to him and stopped him. The pan was full of cabbage, and water bubbling up. If it had gone over him it would have killed him. Nathan's Mum was upstairs.

Derek (aged 9 years):

I was playing in our front garden, and my cousin and my little brother were playing in the front bedroom upstairs. Well, I just looked up and saw smoke coming out of the bedroom window. I ran upstairs, and there was a fire. It was about this high (18 inches). I got a bucket of water and threw it over it. I had to run downstairs — it took three buckets. I think it was a paraffin heater — or something — that caused the fire.

Several other children had equally hair-raising stories to tell, and I realised that there were a number of unsung heroes and heroines in our school community as well as in the "mountains of material" in my book cupboard.

There were one or two worrying episodes involving Sophie Ellwood towards the end of February. On one occasion, she accused a boy in her class of indecently assaulting her in the school playground. Vincent questioned her closely and discovered that during some horseplay, the boy had run past her and pulled at the zip of her skirt. He spoke to the boy about rough, inappropriate behaviour and warned Sophie against exaggeration.

It seemed that the wild accusation had sprung from her past unfortunate experiences, but Vincent sensed that there was agitation and unrest amongst other girls in the class.

About a week later, during the lunch break, several girls in the class, provoked by Sophie's comments about their parents, decided to join together and take their revenge. Only the intervention of three "dinner ladies" prevented a violent attack on her in the playground.

As the teachers had withdrawn from supervising children at lunch time, it was up to me to speak to all the girls and make it clear that their behaviour was unacceptable and must not be repeated. Later, to emphasise the point, Vincent kept the girls inside during the afternoon break.

After school, the father of one of the girls returned to school to complain about this punishment. He said that although it was wrong of his daughter to threaten violence, the real culprit was Sophie Ellwood who, in addition to informing the entire class of her own unfortunate experiences, kept making personal, derogatory remarks about the other children's parents. He felt so strongly about this that he had been to see Sophie's stepmother to protest.

The following morning, I talked again with two girls who appeared to be the ringleaders in the class. I said that although I accepted that they had been provoked, I was not prepared to tolerate violence of any kind in school. From then on there seemed to be an improvement in their behaviour, so much so that one of the "dinner ladies" reported that all the girls were playing together quite happily during lunch breaks.

I was relieved that things had settled down. Violence was unexpected in a primary school — especially amongst girls!

As February came to an end, there was to be a change of staff. Hilary Varley had been employed on a temporary contract at St Marks for almost two years, covering first one and then another of our permanent teachers who went on maternity leave. She herself was now pregnant, so when Cilla Baxter rang to say that she would be able to return to work at the beginning of March, Hilary was able to depart with joy rather than with sadness.

During her final week, the children brought in contributions towards a present for her, and although it was meant to be a secret, one or two children in her class could not resist telling her that she was in for a "surprise" on her last day. This worried Hilary. The thought of a presentation in front of the whole school troubled her. Vincent assured her that the ceremony would involve as little fuss as possible. To fulfil the promise, she was handed a basket of baby items at the end of assembly on the day she was due to leave.

The early days of March brought a number of events giving rise to feelings of frustration, delight, pleasure and elation.

On her first day back at school after maternity leave, Cilla Baxter told me that she and her husband had decided to have a second baby very soon, so she only intended to return to work for thirteen weeks — the minimum period required after claiming paid maternity leave. She would be resigning before the end of the school year — towards the end of May. This meant I would have to appoint a temporary teacher from then until the day we broke up in July — a period of about 8 weeks! The children in the class would undoubtedly suffer, but it was all perfectly legal. I felt frustrated, but there was nothing I could do.

On the following morning, I shared Joe Jackson's delight at the arrival of three gigantic refuse bins which had been delivered to replace our twelve small ones, many of which were battered and lidless as a result of vandalism during the dark winter evenings. After closer examination however, Joe expressed concern.

"They've got wheels on!" he exclaimed, putting his head round my office door at playtime. "I can see that causing trouble — they'll have a field day!"

I agreed. Such a feature was an open invitation to our local youths to use the containers for joyriding, and the sloping school drive would make a perfect track. Joe spent the rest of the day on a quest for a long piece of chain and a padlock in order to anchor the bins to the sturdy fence surrounding the bin area. By evening, all was secure.

A few days later, a large carton was delivered to school, and as it had the word "Office" printed across it, Mrs Mullen and I opened it together. To our great pleasure, it was a brand new ink duplicator which we desperately needed.

For several months, I had been trying to persuade the Supplies Department to replace our 1930's machine with a new model. Our present one had the unfortunate habit of spilling ink and oil over the table and staining Mrs Mullen's hands and clothing whenever she used it.

The main stumbling block had been my insistence that the Local Authority, rather than the school, should pay for it. I argued that a duplicator, being office equipment, (and in the same category as filing cabinets, shelves, and light bulbs) should not be paid for from "educational money". Finally my tenacity had won the day.

March saw the first meeting on our proposed school extension. I was elated. This was the first clear indication that the Local Authority had accepted my claim that one was necessary. Four of us sat around my desk — Derek Edwards, Educational Advisor, Len Bedford, architect, Jack Toogood, project officer, and myself. Our discussion lasted well over an hour, and I was pleased to note that most of my recommendations had been accepted by the rest of the group.

Afterwards, Derek Edwards walked around the classrooms and had conversations with several teachers. He learned that Cilla Baxter had just introduced a theme called "New Life" and was planning an interesting session for her class in two day's time. Before leaving, he told me that he just *had* to return to see what happened as the lesson sounded fascinating!

On the chosen day, Cilla arrived at school very early, accompanied by her five-month-old baby and a mountain of nursery equipment in the back of her car.

When the children came into school, Cilla told them to sit in a semi-circle on the carpet and placed the baby on a rug in front of the group. She then showed the class all the items that had been brought, explaining how each was used and giving demonstrations with the baby's cooperation. Needless to say, this created a tremendous amount of interest and excitement, and the children asked lots of questions which the teacher attempted to answer. Some of the children shared stories about younger brothers and sisters, or family pets, and there was no doubt that they learned a great deal about "New Life."

A few minutes after the lesson began, Derek Edwards arrived and was soon fascinated by the events taking place. Cilla's baby behaved perfectly throughout the entire proceedings — smiling, gurgling and experimenting with her toys — and Derek told me

124

afterwards that he thought the children had benefited greatly from having a living "visual aid"!

Having been the "star" of the morning, Baby Baxter returned home at lunch time to take her afternoon nap.

Early in March, Vincent Leach and Lesley Dunn had begun to plan a cross-country run for the top two classes due to take place just before the school closed for the Easter Holiday. They had plotted a course around a local park and planned a return route across two fields and along the bank of a canal. Although entry into the race was voluntary, it stimulated great interest amongst the children, and almost all of them decided to "have a go".

When the day arrived, Lesley, Diane and I, accompanied by half a dozen parents and 64 children, walked along to the local park, which lay about a mile from school. Vincent was already there and had made careful preparations, ensuring the safety of the route and that no part of it took the children over private land.

They were started off in groups of 8, (with times noted on different stopwatches), and they all set off with enthusiasm. However, the difference in time taken to complete the course between the winners and those bringing up in the rear was remarkable. Two boys from the top class came first in a dead heat and completed the course in less than 15 minutes. The slowest runners took around 20 minutes longer!

The children who ran the course thoroughly enjoyed the experience and, on returning to school at 3.15p.m., were given a sweet for completing it. Easter eggs had been bought as main prizes for the various winners — first boy and girl in each class, etc. — and these were given out during the final assembly before we closed for Easter.

CHAPTER
THIRTEEN

Spring

The Easter holiday was no more restful than the Christmas break had been. My sister and I were in the process of selling Mum's house in Littleborough, and we were all aware that it was the end of an era.

At home, I spent time reading through a great sheaf of forms from applicants hoping to take on Cilla Baxter's job at the end of May. A permanent teacher could not begin work until September, but I needed a temporary teacher to complete the current year.

I was increasingly worried about the effect that the teachers' work-to-rule was having on the school. During recent weeks, I had had to write letters to parents saying that children in certain classes should not be sent to school on particular days, as their teacher was ill and other members of staff were unable to cover for absences. Of course, this had not gone down well and mutterings of resentment could be heard from parents in the playground as they waited to collect their children.

A further problem was on the horizon too. Every year in July, we issued Report Books, which were sent out to parents a few weeks before we broke up for the summer holiday. The following week, we would hold a Parents' Evening in school, at which parents returned the books and met with teachers to discuss their children's progress. This year, as teachers were refusing to do anything that could not take place within the working day, they were unwilling to complete the Report Books, (normally done at home), or return to school for the Parents' Evening. I could foresee that this would create real anger amongst many parents.

Constant anxiety and the drain of supervising school meals every day were beginning to wear me down. I was becoming more and more depressed. Anita decided to take action.

"I've booked a short break to celebrate our anniversary," she announced the day after we had closed for Easter. "Can you remember how many years it is?"

I made a quick calculation.

"Well, as we married on 1st April 1961, it must be 24 years," I replied. "Where are we going?"

"The Grange Hotel in Grange-over-Sands in the southern Lake District. When I told the manager it was our anniversary, he asked if it was a special one. I said we were only one year short of our Silver Wedding — so if it hasn't been especially requested by a bridal couple, he has agreed to put us in the Honeymoon Suite!"

The manager was true to his word. A few days later found us in a lovely room on the top floor of the hotel, with a panoramic view of the bay. Spread out before us were the hotel gardens and, in the distance, the main street of Grange, with its Victorian arcades and floral displays. The food was excellent, the scenery magnificent and the weather kind. We were able to do lots of walking, and I was able to cast off the pressures of work for a few days.

Once back home, I was brought down to earth with a bump! Newspaper headlines were full of the teachers' industrial action.

"Classroom chaos is forecast as the teachers' work-to-rule policy begins to bite," they screamed. "Pupils are facing being sent home from school or missing lessons because of the "no cover" industrial action which members of the National Union of Teachers launched on February 6th.

Teachers are refusing to cover for absent colleagues, carry out dinner duties, or do any other work out of school hours, in protest at the Government's four per cent pay offer."

There seemed no end in sight to the industrial action. I would have to cope with it until the end of the school year.

On 15th April, within the first hour of the Summer term, Vincent informed me that in a few days time he would be going into hospital for treatment on his eye. Once again I contacted Brenda Pilling to put her on "stand-by".

Towards the end the week, I joined Lesley Dunn, Diane Davies and Ken Bowdler — a friend of Janet Clarke — who were taking Primary 5 children on an educational visit to Settlewood. Before I became head in 1974, the annual school trips were largely "fun days out" to celebrate the end of the academic year — reminiscent of Sunday school outings when everyone piled into a coach and went off to the seaside for the day.

As part of a thematic approach to teaching, however, classes of children were now taken on a number of shorter trips each year which, as well as being enjoyable, included a learning experience. For example, children learning about the emergency services might be taken on a half-day visit to a fire station, or pupils studying the industrial revolution could be taken to a cotton mill museum. If the subject of the theme was farming, a visit to a local farm was often arranged, and Egyptian mummies, fossils or dinosaur skeletons could always be viewed at a city centre museum nearby.

In the case of Primary 5, the children had been learning about modes of transport through the ages. Their educational visit was to Settlewood where there was a canal. On the day in question, having collected our packed lunches from Chef, we enjoyed a pleasant half-hour trip by coach, and were dropped off close to the Settlewood Canal. The children were excited to see a narrow boat drawn up alongside the landing stage, and Mr Newall, the owner of the boat, greeted the children cheerfully. Soon we were chugging slowly along the 2 mile stretch of recently restored waterway, whilst the "captain" gave a running commentary on things to look out for and the reasons for his various manoeuvres.

130

During the ninety-minute sail, we negotiated two locks and traversed an aqueduct. The children were fascinated by all aspects of the voyage — especially the passage through the locks — and asked lots of questions which Mr Newall cheerfully answered. By the time the journey ended, at the same spot from which it had begun, the children had learned a great deal and worked up an appetite. We sat on a flight of steps in the canal-side park to eat our sandwiches before sharing any leftover crusts with the ducks!

After lunch, the children went into the nearby Settlewood Museum, where we were welcomed by the Museum Education Officer. She talked to the children about what they had learned from their morning sail, and then explained the layout of the rooms and the various displays connected with the canal. The children were given worksheets and moved about in groups studying exhibits, copying information, and trying to wheedle the answers to difficult questions out of Lesley and Diane!

At 2.30p.m., we boarded the coach and half an hour later arrived back at St Marks after a successful and interesting day. I always found such visits brought a subject to life!

The days of April passed quickly. Vincent was admitted to hospital and returned a week later having undergone further tests. Jack Toogood, the school project officer, came in with the news that the proposed extension had been put back by a year. Interviews were held to appoint a replacement for Cilla Baxter.

One sunny morning, I arrived at school and was taking my customary walk around the classrooms when I came upon Joe Jackson wrapping strips of crepe paper round a portable netball post.

I looked at him in surprise.

"Do you know what day it is?" he asked abruptly.

"Er . . . Wednesday."

"It's *May Day*! I was telling Miss Clarke yesterday, children are missing out on *everything* nowadays."

"Oh, it's a maypole!"

Joe gave me a withering look.

"That's right. Miss Clarke said that if I could make a maypole by today, the Infants would hold a May Day festival this afternoon."

I continued on my tour thinking of the truth of what he had said. We had tended to ignore May Day along with other traditional ceremonies as they seemed inappropriate for our children, raised in an urban environment in the age of television. I came upon Janet and Cathy looking at books in Janet's Homebase, and told them what Joe had said and what he was making.

"Oh, we know all about it!" exclaimed Cathy with a grin. "He buttonholed us as soon as we came in this morning!"

They showed me a very old book that Janet had unearthed containing photographs of May Day celebrations in an English village in the 1930s and, inspired by this they were hurriedly rearranging their afternoon programme to include songs and dances around the maypole.

132

In the joint assembly that morning, I found myself —
with very little preparation — talking about the end of
winter and the advent of spring and explaining how, for
centuries, rural folk had welcomed the coming season
with a May Day party on the village green. During the
afternoon, Janet came to my office to invite me to
crown the May Queen — and May King! — who were
to preside over the singing and dancing by Primaries 1
and 2 in the school hall. Great fun was had by all!

After school, several members of staff said how sad it
was that today there were so few community
celebration events. Janet suggested that perhaps in the
future our school should try to become more involved
in the community life of our district.

Joe said little about the events of the day, but he was
obviously delighted that his input had been accepted
and acted upon so swiftly by the teachers.

The days were now lengthening, and often there was a
feeling of spring in the air. Terry Jones, the regular
deputy head, came into school a few times, causing
great excitement amongst the children, who were
pleased to see him. As part of his B.Ed. course, he was
carrying out a piece of research into some aspect of
mathematics.

We also had a visit from Gordon Letts, a fund raiser
for the northern region of the Royal National Institute
for the Blind, who had been a regular visitor to St
Marks for several years. He spoke to the juniors during
morning assembly, and produced from his case several
interesting items.

The first was a Braille typewriter on which he typed the Braille alphabet as the children called out the letters, and he also showed them a Braille *Radio Times* and the first volume of the Concise Oxford Dictionary which in all ran to 15 volumes! Next he produced a child's ball which emitted a continuous bleeping tone so it could be located; a device which enabled a blind person to pour a cup of tea without spilling it; a collapsible white walking stick; and a "talking" watch which told him the time in a robotic voice — much to the children's amusement.

Before leaving, Mr Letts left some gift envelopes for the children to take home and said he would willingly return to receive the donation if there was a good response.

Throughout the year, we would be approached by a number of charities wanting to tell the children about their work, hoping to raise money for their cause. The decision was mine on which to allow into school and which to refuse.

There were also groups who offered some sort of "educational experience". In this category came puppeteers who gave a performance and then spent a few minutes showing the children how to make their own puppet from a wooden spoon, and the Punch and Judy man who talked about the history of the play for a few moments before disappearing into his striped, upright tent. These groups had to be booked in advance and a fee had to be paid.

Then there were agencies which visited schools as part of their work. The police came to talk about road safety and supervise the Cycling Proficiency Course; firemen came to talk about preventing fires in the home; doctors or nurses came to carry out medical examinations (not easy in an open plan school!) or check the children's hair; dentists came to demonstrate how to brush teeth and horrify the children with pictures of neglected mouths.

On one occasion, two visiting train drivers impressed on the children the dangers of playing on railway lines. Both admitted to killing someone whilst driving a train — a fact that made the children's mouths drop open. But the message went home!

As head, I had to take care not to overload the system — it would have been easy to have a procession of visitors every week!

Towards the end of May, Anita and I had just finished Sunday lunch when the telephone rang. It was Joe Jackson.

"We're in a right bloody mess, here," he said. "Someone broke into the school kitchen last night and threw food and equipment all over the floor."

"Oh, no!"

"That's not the worst of it. They turned on all the cold taps and left them running. When I got here half an hour ago, the kitchen, the school hall, a stock room and part of a class area were under half an inch of water."

135

Within the hour I had joined Joe at St Marks and begun to assess what needed to be done so that the school could open as usual on the following morning. Joe offered to stay and do what was necessary to make the school habitable, and I promised to make sure he got overtime payments for the extra hours he worked. I telephoned Chef, who said he would come in straight away to sterilise the cutlery and utensils ready for lunch on the following day.

I reported the incident to the Education Office first thing the next morning and they sent a building officer to the school immediately. Joe had spent 6 hours moving furniture and equipment, drying the floor to the best of his ability, and then replacing the items in their original position. However, several sections of the parquet floor in the school hall had been raised by the water and, as the blocks had swollen, it would not be possible to re-lay them for a week or two. The building officer arranged for workmen to remove sections of tiles and temporarily replace them with sheets of plywood of the same thickness.

We got through the week somehow and fortunately, on the following Friday, the school broke up for half-term holiday. This gave Joe five clear days in which to move the furniture again, continue the drying process, and then return everything to its proper place before we all returned for the last half of the summer term.

I breathed a sigh of relief as I arrived home on the Friday evening, looking forward to a restful week ahead.

"This has been the worst year of my career so far," I said to Anita. "There's just one half-term to go — I can't wait for the long summer break!"

"It'll probably be all plain sailing from now on," she replied optimistically.

But she couldn't have been more wrong.

CHAPTER
FOURTEEN

The Final Lap

As soon as I walked into school after the holiday, Joe proudly led me into the hall to view the newly re-laid parquet floor which gleamed under three coats of varnish. A team of workmen had arrived during the half-term break and worked hard to finish the job before the children returned. Good news at last!

At lunch time however, Janet confirmed that members of the NUT were not willing to complete their children's Report Books in their own time, so they could not be sent home during the final half term. Teachers who were *not* members of the NUT had decided to complete the books as usual. This meant that some children would take home an end-of-year report whilst others would not. After some thought, I decided to issue *all* the Report Books, enclosing a note of explanation in those that were blank. I would write my usual comments in *every* book in the space marked: "Head Teacher's Remarks". In the circumstances, it was the best I could do.

We had been at school for only a few days when I received a worrying telephone call from the father of a girl in the top class. He apologised for disturbing me, but expressed concern about stories that his daughter had told at home about Vincent's behaviour in class, which seemed to him to be "over-familiar". He had already spoken to the mothers of several other girls in the class, all of whom seemed to corroborate his daughter's tales. He had rung to tell me that three of the mothers had decided to come into school to see me at 8.30a.m. on the following day.

I got very little sleep that night and arrived at school very early — but the expected visitors did not arrive. At 8.40a.m., I received a second telephone call from the father saying that one mother had made an official complaint to the police, and that the matter was now in their hands. I was stunned. I could hardly take in what I was hearing!

I decided I needed all the advice I could get, so before 9 o'clock, I telephoned the Chief Education Officer, Derek Edwards our educational advisor, Reverend Strong, and the local secretary of the National Association of Headteachers to report what had happened. Reverend Strong, who lived close by at the vicarage set off to school immediately to give support, and arrived just as the morning bell sounded and the children came into school.

It soon became apparent that more than half of the children in the top class had been kept at home by their parents as only 15 came into the Homebase. Alarmed and puzzled, Vincent came to my office to see if I knew where the rest of his children were.

I swiftly arranged for Janet to cover for Vincent, took him into the office, closed the door and suggested that he sat down. Then Reverend Strong and I told him of the accusation that had been made against him. He was devastated by the allegations and came very close to tears as he protested his innocence.

Within half an hour we were joined by a senior education officer and a union representative and the "approved procedure" got underway. A statement was taken from me regarding the complaint and Vincent was given the opportunity to answer the allegations. Eventually, because the police had been involved and would undoubtedly be making enquiries, he was suspended from duty with immediate effect — initially for 14 days, but with the possibility of an extension if enquiries were not completed in that time.

Once the formalities were over, Vincent had to gather up all his belongings and leave the premises immediately — a procedure which to me seemed cold, clinical and heartless. The senior education officer advised that if questions were asked by parents, visitors or the press I should make a simple factual statement and give no personal opinion.

An hour later, with everyone gone, Reverend Strong and I sat and stared at each other in disbelief. How could this have happened? It was like the most terrible of nightmares. We did not have long to reflect on the situation, because the rest of the day was taken up with a series of telephone calls and visits from parents which kept us both fully occupied. Reverend Strong stayed with me all day — for which I was very grateful. During the afternoon I had the difficult task of drafting a note to the parents of Vincent's class stating that he would be absent for some time, and another teacher would be replacing him.

Later, I rang the Staffing Section at the Education Office urgently requesting a supply teacher to take the top class on the following day — and possibly for the next two weeks!

"Mmmm . . . not sure about that," replied the clerk, unaware of the great difficulty I was in. "All of our regulars are working in schools at the moment. I'll ring around and see what I can do to help. If I find someone I'll tell them to report to you at school tomorrow morning. Is that O.K?"

I don't know what I replied. I just know that I went home feeling utterly dejected, without knowing how on earth this vulnerable class was to be taught during the next day and the coming weeks.

Anita sat and listened intently whilst I went through the events of the day.

"What could possibly have happened to cause this?" she asked when I had told her the story.

I shook my head. "It's an open plan school! Vincent's Homebase is right next to Lesley Dunn's. They can see each other working for most of the day. If anything inappropriate was happening, surely someone would have noticed it."

It only occurred to me much later that Sophie Ellwood had regaled other children with details of her own unfortunate experiences. They had been given information beyond their years and understanding, and this might have affected their perception of Vincent's words and actions.

"What will happen to Vincent now?" asked Anita.

"I don't know. He's been sent home on full pay, presumably waiting for police investigations to begin. I'll ring him tomorrow to give him moral support — but practically speaking, there's nothing I can do to help."

"What about the class?"

"I've asked the Education Office for a supply teacher from tomorrow, but they're not sure that one is available . . ."

We talked for the whole evening, covering the same ground and asking the same questions over and over again — and getting nowhere. Eventually we went to bed, but neither of us slept very well that night.

Fortunately a supply teacher arrived — but only to cover the next three days, and thankfully Reverend Strong joined me once more to lend his support.

I was very glad to have him with me as my first visitor of the day was a father who had come to complain that he was "very dissatisfied" with the education his daughter had received during the last year. I felt sure that he was capitalizing on our present unfortunate situation, as his daughter had one of the poorest attendance records in the school, and was already having extra help with reading. I decided to attack rather than defend.

"Mr Garston," I began. "We have just completed a series of standardised tests throughout the school, and I can assure you that our results are very good. Some children did very well indeed. Of course, there are one or two pupils who are rather slower learners, but that is to be expected in any school.

"Would you like to discuss your own daughter's progress? It is true that Carla *is* one of the slower learners, but she does have a *very* poor attendance record. It might be helpful for us to look at the attendance register together. Then perhaps I could suggest ways in which you could help her at home and tell you about the ways we are trying to help her here."

Mr Garston back-pedalled rapidly.

"Oh no," he muttered apprehensively. "I know Carla has had quite a lot of time off school . . ."

As the parent got to his feet and edged towards the door, Reverend Strong spoke for the first time.

"As Chairman of the School Governors," he said, "I advise you to put your complaint in writing and hand it to me personally. I will make sure it is considered by the Governing Body."

"Right," said Mr Garston, and disappeared through the doorway.

I was glad we had seen off this troublemaker. The school had always had an "open door" policy, with parents welcome to discuss at any time their child's progress with me or their child's teacher. There are times when we have to make a stand — and this was such a time.

* * *

That evening, I returned to school for a Governors' Meeting. Chairman Reverend Strong was already aware of the allegations of the last two days, but I had to inform the rest of the Governors that Vincent had been suspended and that police enquiries were being made. We then proceeded with the rest of the business in a rather subdued mood — my news had thrown a damper over the whole meeting.

The next morning, as soon as I got into school, I received a call from the senior education officer who had supervised the procedure when Vincent was suspended. He had just read the minutes of the previous night's meeting and immediately launched into a personal attack on me.

"In spite of my warning, you have informed parents that Mr Leach has been suspended," he said. "And you've mentioned the matter to the Governing Body!"

He went on to say that this was a serious breach of discipline, and that he would have to bring the matter before the Chief Education Officer. He advised me to contact my union representative.

I was shaken and dismayed by his aggressive attitude. I believed that I had acted responsibly throughout the entire affair. I had not felt able to go through a 2 hour meeting with the School Governors — on the day following the suspension — without even mentioning it and believed it only sensible to notify parents if their child's teacher was likely to be absent for a considerable time, especially as they already knew the reason for his absence!

I contacted my union representative who suggested that I write out a full account of the affair, detailing the events in school and my actions. Having reflected on the matter for a day or two, I also wrote to the senior education officer concerned. I asked him when, where and in whose presence he had warned me not to *mention* the matter to parents or the Governing Body, as it was my recollection that he had warned me not to *express an opinion* about it. I heard no more about the matter!

In subsequent days the whole school seemed to be under a cloud. Teachers walked around with serious faces and there was a deep sense of heaviness and foreboding in the air.

Then came the revival!

On the Monday morning of the following week, Harriet Carr arrived. She was an experienced teacher and had been appointed by the Education Office as a "permanent supply teacher" to take Vincent's class until he returned — whenever that might be! She had prepared a great deal of rather formal work for the class, and during the next few days the children spent the greater part of each day with their noses to the grindstone. It was a wise approach and just what was needed. The class settled down in record time!

A few days later, the teachers of classes 1, 2 and 3 suggested that their pupils would benefit from — and enjoy — a visit to Blackpool Zoo. I agreed immediately. The diary was studied and a date fixed in mid-July. At first the cost of hiring a coach seemed prohibitive, but the helpful proprietor suggested a double-deck coach which could hold 70 adults, and therefore over 90 small children. (Seat belts were not required in those days). The total charge would be £125.

That Friday afternoon, I rang Vincent once more to see how he was faring. He told me he felt better as each day passed, although he still had an underlying anxiety about the allegations. He had heard nothing "official" since his suspension, and had not even been asked to give a statement to the police.

CHAPTER
FIFTEEN

The Finishing Line

The school year was drawing to an end. It was early July, and the finishing line was in sight. I spent a couple of hours every evening writing comments in the end-of-year report books. Those issued to pupils in Primaries 2, 4 and 5 contained no marks or teacher assessments, in line with union recommendations.

I wrote a short comment at the foot of the page in books that had been completed by the teachers, and a longer, fuller comment in those that were otherwise blank. In addition I enclosed a note with each report stating that there were to be no parent/teacher interviews at the end of the term.

A week later came the day of the eagerly anticipated trip. Children from Primaries 1, 2 and 3, accompanied by eight adults, were setting off on a full day visit to Blackpool Zoo. When I arrived at school at 8.20a.m., the teachers were already there, assembling boxes of towels, first aid materials and paper handkerchiefs. By the time most of the pupils had arrived at 8.50a.m., everything was ready and stacked neatly by the front door.

In addition to the teachers and two parents, three other helpers had joined the party, including one of our school governors.

"Chef" had prepared packed lunches for all the children and when the double-deck coach arrived at the school gates at 9.10a.m., Joe Jackson ferried the boxes of food and supplies out to it. Excited pupils boarded the bus and within 5 minutes it was pulling away, each of its windows framing two or more enthusiastic faces.

When the party returned at 3.50p.m., a group of happy adults and children spilled out on to the pavement to be greeted by a cluster of waiting mothers. The smiling faces of the adults showed that the trip had been successful and this was confirmed by the teachers when they came into school. The zoo part of the visit had been very popular, and the trip to a beach after lunch had been most enjoyable. Many of the children had paddled in the sea — and one or two adults had joined them! By all accounts, the visit had been completely satisfactory from first to last, for which I felt immensely thankful.

I exchanged a few words with Janet before she left for home.

"I'm *so* glad that this event was successful," she said, "because after the things that have happened in school recently, I don't think I could have coped with failure."

Her words expressed my feelings exactly.

On opening the school mail on the following day, I was surprised to find an envelope containing a £5 note, accompanied by a letter expressing appreciation of the time and effort given by the staff for the benefit of the children. I felt cheered by the gift, acknowledged it and later came across a list of the school's giving to charity during the previous few months. Since September, St Marks had given £143 to Christian Aid for help in the Ethiopian famine, and £151 to the Royal National Institute for the Blind.

That afternoon, pupils from Primaries 3 and 4, Primary 5 Recorder Group, three teachers and I walked to the Jerusalem Social Centre, a quarter of a mile away, to entertain a group of "senior citizens". When we arrived, we were ushered into a large room around which 80 or 90 elderly people were seated at small tables. The room was very warm, and the atmosphere smoky, but nevertheless the children performed very well. Their songs had been learned during music lessons and were sung with gusto! The Recorder Group played popular tunes such as *My Old Man Said Follow the Van* and *The Skye Boat Song* and the audience joined in heartily with the words. After much applause, the children were rewarded with orange juice and biscuits, and we set off back to school. Janet Clarke had been especially pleased with the children's performance, so yet again a day closed on a positive note.

The final week of the school year had arrived at last.

We had planned to hold our traditional Sports Afternoon on Tuesday, but torrential rain swept across the school field for most of the day so we had to postpone it.

Wednesday morning dawned fine, but heavy clouds and wet grass made it appear unlikely that the event could go ahead. At eleven o'clock the clouds parted, the sun shone brightly, the temperature rose by several degrees and the field began to dry. By lunchtime, the sky was bright blue. Summer had reappeared.

The staff and I decided to take action, and with the help of the older juniors, chairs, ropes, hoops and all the other paraphernalia were carried out to the field and by 2 o'clock the "Sports Afternoon" was underway.

The events were simple, and the fifty-minute programme ran smoothly. Each class participated in a sprint, and a variety of novelty races — egg and spoon, three-legged, bean-bag between knees, etc. — which produced much delight and laughter. Local parents, attracted by the activity on the field, came in to watch the events, and a pleasant afternoon was had by all.

The day was only marred by one or two parents who, disappointed at having missed the impromptu Sports Afternoon, arrived at school at 3.30p.m. and began to complain loudly and bitterly within the hearing of the teachers. Diane, Cathy and Janet were put out by their comments, but Janet was particularly hurt by their pointed remarks about "teachers who cannot even be bothered to write a few lines on a report" — referring to the industrial action. The parents concerned appeared to be more upset by the fact that they had missed *watching* the Sports Afternoon, than pleased that the staff had put in a lot of effort so that their children would not be disappointed.

On the last day of the school year, Reverend Strong came in to take the morning assembly. He told a story directed at the children, some a little tearful, who would be leaving the school that day. It was about a caterpillar which struggled with inevitable changes but was finally transformed into a butterfly and flew off into the sunshine.

Then came a surprise — at least for Diane Davies, who was to be married during the summer holiday! For several weeks, children and staff had been secretly contributing towards a present for her.

The presentation took place at the close of the assembly. I made a suitable short speech, and Diane came to the front of the hall to be presented with a colourfully wrapped cardboard box — produced by Cathy from behind the piano! Diane made a great show, for the benefit of the children, of removing the wrapping paper, to reveal a china tea-service which had been bought for her. Several pupils had brought in their own presents for Diane, and came out to give her those. The occasion was rounded off by a whole school rendering of one of Diane's favourite songs.

At lunchtime, we enjoyed a buffet lunch arranged for us by Janet. Each of us had contributed towards the cost, and a spread of open sandwiches, salads, flans and gateaux was enjoyed by all — including Reverend Strong and Terry Jones, our soon-to-return deputy head, who had joined us for the occasion.

At last it was home time and the children hurried out, joyous at the anticipation of six weeks of fun and games. I said goodbye to Joe, wished members of staff a restful and happy holiday and got into my car, which was already loaded with books, files and schemes of work that needed my attention during the summer holiday.

The year had been a difficult one; but at last it was over.

Anita welcomed me home with a big hug.

"Six whole weeks before you need to think about school again!" she said cheerfully, knowing that that was very unlikely to be the case. A glance at my bulging brief case which I had put down in a corner confirmed it!

The events of the last few months had set me thinking, and those thoughts had now crystallised into an intention. It was obvious to me that working in schools was becoming increasingly difficult — for two main reasons as I saw it. The first was that many children were growing up in less stable homes, were less well disciplined on entry and were more assertive than in previous generations. The second reason was that educational bureaucracy was more complex, more remote, and less caring and supportive in its dealings with employees.

Teachers were caught in a trap. They had been stripped of authority, felt demoralised and underpaid, yet were expected to carry out their role with increasing expertise, efficiency and responsibility.

My position as a head teacher during the last year had been intolerable. For much of the time, I had been without a deputy, through illness, then suspension; I had been forced to cope with a withdrawal of goodwill by the teachers (on instruction from their Union) which had left me unable to hold staff meetings, arrange parents' evenings or issue school reports; and I had been obliged to supervise school meals every day since early February.

My initial enthusiasm for the job had been diminishing for some time. The hope that I was doing something worthwhile and making a real difference in children's lives had disappeared. The tree which had budded in my youth and blossomed in my middle years was now bearing bitter fruit.

Throughout the years of our marriage, Anita had tended to be optimistic and positive, seeing the cup as half full, whereas too often I saw it as half empty. I didn't know how she would react to my next words.

"There's something we need to talk about," I said. "I think it's time for me to strike out in a new direction. I need to look for another job."

Postscript

No charges were ever brought against Vincent Leach. The police decided there was no case to answer and eventually he continued with his career in teaching — but not, of course, at St Marks, as his year as Acting Deputy Head had come to an end. In retrospect, it seems likely that the effects of Sophie Ellwood's sexual awareness precipitated the accusation against him and caused the hysterical reaction of several other girls in the class. Hopefully, today, Sophie and her family would receive better support and counselling.

I heard nothing more from the senior education officer about my so-called "breach of discipline" in disclosing Vincent's suspension to the Governing Body and the parents. However, my self-confidence had been severely shaken by the episode, as I believed I had acted properly throughout.

It was this school year — 1984/5 — which spurred me on to leave the profession I had once found so fulfilling. However, over the next two years, I was to discover that the skills developed over 30 years in teaching do not transfer easily to other occupations and for some time I had to soldier on.

In 1987, the awaited work on the extension began, providing a more appropriate staff room with a large stockroom attached, a cloakroom for the older pupils, and a changing room with a shower block for children taking part in outdoor games and football matches.

Also in 1987, possibly in response to teachers' continued unrest and industrial action, the government introduced "Teachers' Directed Time". This required teachers, (other than head teachers and deputy head teachers whose work commitment remained "open"), to work 1265 "directed" hours per annum, and to be available for work on 195 days in any school year. This legal requirement radically changed the attitude of many teachers, most of whom — up to this point — had voluntarily given many hours of their "own time" to improve and enrich their pupils' education. There were now fewer after-school sports fixtures and fewer lunch-time clubs. It changed too the nature of the relationship between head and staff in primary schools. Instead of being a senior teacher leading a team, the head now became viewed as the "school manager" and the teachers as "the workforce".

The ethos of the school had radically changed.

In 1988, the National Curriculum was to be introduced into primary and secondary state schools in England, Wales and Northern Ireland, bringing with it another burden of overload and stress. Fortunately for me, before it was implemented, the opportunity arose to take early retirement. I grasped it with both hands and the following year signed on as a student at Sheffield University. There I retrained and became a personal counsellor.

Also available in ISIS Large Print:

Kept in Czech

Margaret Austin

"Once in the dance hall for the second Saturday running I scanned the crowd in search of the Little Czech, as I had heard him referred to by another student who was also obviously quite smitten with him."

Margaret had just arrived in Leicester to begin her English course at the University College (as it then was), when she saw Fred and thought, "You look as though you're used to getting your own way, but you're not going to get me!" How wrong she was! Three weeks later they were firmly involved with each other and have remained so for 61 years (so far!). Almost immediately, Fred was totally accepted into Margaret's family and her home became his home.

ISBN 978-0-7531-9564-2 (hb)
ISBN 978-0-7531-9565-9 (pb)

Czech and Mate

Fred Austin

"I suppose that I had always (In my youthful experience!) been attracted by the smaller, darker-haired girls: they fitted better when you danced."

Fred saw Margaret for the first time in the queue for the Dean at the University College, Leicester. The year was 1947. He was making a fresh start and liked what he saw, noticing her little zipped dress.

His mother had sent him to England, at the age of ten, to escape the Nazis. Before 1939, Fred had lived happily with his mother and two sisters in Northern Moravia. Once in England, he soon adapted to a life, which was happy in school, but far from normal otherwise.

In meeting Margaret Fred was, at last, encouraged to fulfil his potential and was able, in spite of setbacks to his health, to contribute to the life they made together.

ISBN 978-0-7531-9562-8 (hb)
ISBN 978-0-7531-9563-5 (pb)